Arranging Flowers

THE BEST OF MARTHA STEWART LIVING

Arranging Flowers

How to Create Beautiful Bouquets in Every Season

Clarkson Potter/Publishers
New York

Originally published in book form by
Martha Stewart Living Omnimedia LLC
in 1999. Published simultaneously by
Clarkson N. Potter, Inc.,
Oxmoor House, Inc., and Leisure Arts.

A portion of this work was previously
published in MARTHA STEWART LIVING.

Published by Clarkson N. Potter, Inc.,
201 East 50th Street, New York, NY 10022.
Member of the Crown Publishing Group.
Random House, Inc. New York, Toronto,
London, Sydney, Auckland
www.randomhouse.com
Clarkson N. Potter, Potter, and
colophon are registered trademarks
of Random House, Inc.

Printed in the United States of America.

Library of Congress Cataloging-in-
Publication Data is available upon request.

ISBN 0-609-80361-1

10 9 8 7 6 5 4 3 2 1
First Edition

Senior Editor: Bruce Shostak
Art Director: Linda Kocur
Writer: James A. Baggett
Managing Editor: Molly Gregor Tully
Design Production Associate: Curtis Smith
Assistant Art Director: Jill Groeber

contents

introduction

One of the greatest pleasures I know is the pleasure of arranging flowers. To experience the joy of handling nature's precious gifts of colorful, scented, extraordinary blooms and to coax them into displays of unparalleled, albeit confined, beauty is for me akin to picking up a paintbrush and capturing their vibrant glory in the style of great still lifes by Redon, Matisse, or Bonnard.

Walking through my garden, I am constantly amazed by the bounty that a bit of intense gardening will provide. From late winter, when the oddly colored hellebores peep out from a dusting of snow, to latest autumn, when rose hips glisten in the pelting rain, there are so many materials that demand inclusion in arrangements.

I was four when I made my first flower arrangement. We had just moved from a small apartment in Jersey City, New Jersey, which had no yard, to the Elm Place house in Nutley that would become our family home and garden. I was allowed to pick the early tulips that Dad had planted the year before and place them carefully in a vase. Dad watched every move, and told me about height and width and proper containers. I was his willing student and assistant. The garden was mostly for vegetables for

Mother's kitchen, but ample space was allotted for many flowers—everything from tulips and daffodils to sturdy roses, zinnias, marigolds, cosmos, lilies, and many asters, my father's favorite cut flower. It was my job to weed the flower beds, fill the empty spots with annual seedlings that Dad grew on our kitchen windowsill, deadhead spent blooms, and cut the perfect flowers for arrangements. All season long there were flowers on the piano, on the dining table, and in the kitchen. Everyone made a fuss about the flowers. And every one of the six Kostyra children learned the names—common and botanical—of each variety. To this day we can recite them as we walk through any garden, anywhere.

I have tried to pass along this affection for flowers to my own daughter, and I know I have succeeded, for she now surpasses me in her creative techniques. Alexis enjoys her early morning forays in the rose garden, snipping the prettiest blooms while pruning and deadheading so that the blooming continues. And I know she is a real aficionado because she is now asking for more Casablanca lily bulbs, more colors of hydrangeas, and more varieties of viburnum so that she can vary her arrangements.

I have kept secret the fact that I recently planted a thousand more tulips in the East Hampton garden. I know she will be the first to see them in the spring and will use their blooms to great advantage in the many containers she has assiduously collected.

And really, that's what this book is about: the joy of growing, nurturing, and choosing flowers outdoors, or of buying them in a market (one certainly doesn't need a garden to enjoy arranging flowers), so that they can be enjoyed indoors. Flower arranging is an art, but it is so much more. It is developing an eye for beautiful combinations of colors and textures. It is choosing the best vase for the flowers. It is knowing how to prepare cut flowers and how to secure them—using frogs, wire, tape, or clay—so that the arrangements last their longest and won't tilt or topple.

I and everyone who worked on this book hope that each one of you who uses it finds inspiration and encouragement and instruction in its pages. We loved creating the book, and we hope you love using it.

Martha Stewart

The Basics of Arranging

Making the

most beautiful,

longest-lasting

bouquets begins

with understanding

a few simple

principles—and

putting some florists'

tricks to work

Martha's approach to flowers—from growing, cutting, buying, and conditioning them to designing and caring for a lovely arrangement— epitomizes her great

passion for gardening and natural beauty. "Flowers," she says, "belong everywhere, in every nook and cranny of a house." For Martha, that may mean masses of flowers in the entry hall to brighten winter's chilly shadows, or a little jar filled with spring violets set on a laundry-room shelf.

Blooms change from season to season— and from garden to garden—but Martha keeps the same considerations always in mind. She looks carefully at the flowers' shapes and the stems' basic characteristics. She evaluates the setting for the flowers as well as the choice of container. She follows some basic principles gleaned from her own experience and from years of working with professional floral designers. And she never fights intuition. When arranging flowers, you, too, should trust your intuition. But the art is less a guessing game and more a logical process when you know the principles and easy techniques on the following pages—and understand a little of the rich past of flower arranging.

Styles of floral displays have changed from era to era. The ancient Egyptians favored containers in the shape of a pedestal; they also wore flowers as personal

adornment. The ancient Greeks preferred their displays in garlands of laurel or grape leaves. Fashioned into wreaths to symbolize victory, the decorations were placed on the heads of heroes and statues of deities. A more stylized form of display that included nuts, fruits, berries, and ornamental foliage in opulent arrangements emerged during the Renaissance. Seventeenth-century Flemish and Dutch masters depicted in their paintings the ultimate in naturalistic botanical perfection: brightly colored, mixed arrangements—including insects— that were freely styled.

With the Victorian era came newly hybridized plants and a complex, coded language of flowers. In a beribboned posy of fragrant blossoms, called a tussy mussy, each flower carried a special meaning, conveying romantic messages to the recipient. In the 1930s, legendary English floral designer Constance Spry took on the ambitious task of teaching rules and guidelines of domestic floral design. Her concepts of style, form, structure, balance, harmony, and rhythm incorporated a wide array of exotic and familiar materials, including fruits and vegetables. The 1970s

Equipped with a selection of vases, tools, and techniques, you'll find great flexibility in arranging flowers. Sometimes it's as simple as parading individual peonies (previous spread) in glass cordials. Displays of more stems may need the support of a floral frog, like these vintage ones (left), or of other materials, like a screen of chicken wire (above). Even containers that are not meant for flowers (below), like compotes and pitchers, can become a very useful collection of vases.

was the era of the monster stalk, a single stem rising imperiously from a dry bed of moss or a globe filled with water.

Like most pleasures these days—cooking, eating, entertaining—flower arranging has loosened up. Today we are more apt to choose flowers that can be gathered in abundance from the garden and displayed casually in a favorite container. The greatest challenge in arranging flowers is creating an effect of elegance—a silver julep cup filled with pansies, a cut-glass compote brimming with peonies. The secret, of course, is to make it all look effortless.

For Martha, flower arranging begins in her garden. She starts by asking, "What do I have, how much do I have, and how best can I show it off?" As much as possible, Martha tries not to mix cuttings from florists or other gardens in order to avoid losing a certain natural vitality in her arrangements. Each pass through Martha's cutting garden reflects the hues and shades particular to each season—and particular to the flowers she chooses to plant each year. But Martha certainly does not restrict her picking to the cutting garden; she will harvest almost any flower from her gardens that catches her

fancy. So throughout the year, each display of fresh flowers Martha fashions infuses the energy of the season into her homes.

Flowers represent Mother Nature's handiwork at its finest and deserve to be experienced intimately. Every arrangement provides us with the opportunity to study their intriguing nuances—their shapes, colors, textures, and fragrances. Even if you've never arranged flowers before, you will soon discover that nothing is more charming than a small arrangement in an interesting container or more elegant than a single flower in the perfect vase. The rest is up to you and your imagination.

martha's favorite styles

Over the years, Martha has recognized that her arrangements tend to take shape in one of six basic styles: "domed," a display of blooms in an arching mass; "free-form," with flowers that reach and bend; "spiky," which respects blooms that grow on pointy, upright stems, like gladioli and foxgloves; "grouped," or an arrangement made of several small arrangements; "single," the solitary bloom shown to dramatic effect; and "floating," where each bloom sits tranquilly on the surface of water. Usually, the nature of a flower's stem and its blossom shape will tell you what it wants to do, but sometimes, by changing the length of the stem or by massing many flowers into a bouquet, you can explore a flower's personality. Martha's goal is to create arrangements that look as natural as possible.

Once you know these styles, flower arranging is demystified. Consider a solitary peony, fully opened, its stem cut short and set in a cup. The arrangement, "single" and "domed," is perfection on a small scale. In a large vase, several dozen roses might also form a dome—essentially, it's the same arrangement, only reinterpreted, magnified, perhaps in a range of colors.

These styles—shown on the following pages—are central to understanding Martha's personal, sometimes iconoclastic, approach to arranging fresh flowers. Late in May, for example, Martha might gather several dozen Siberian irises; instead of letting them spread out in a large vase, she'll mass them in a dense, many-petaled dome of deep purple. In July, when her gardens supply bushels of roses, she might arrange small cascading sprays with sprigs of flowering herbs; garden roses' wiry stems and floppy habit create a free-form effect. In December, in preparation for the holidays, Martha will gather evergreens and berries to make a spiky display for a hallway table.

What are the rules for color? According to Martha, "no colors clash." But she prefers to keep color pairings uncomplicated. She'll often use a limited color range—for example, pale pink through magenta—or combine complementary colors: whites and greens, purples and pinks, yellows and greens. Martha typically avoids high contrasts, which can end up looking static. Instead, she'll place six or seven yellow flowers in a vase, then add two orange ones to lend richness and depth. It's that simple.

the domed arrangement *Roses from the more than three hundred bushes that fill Martha's East Hampton garden are constructed to form the fullest dome. By using a spherical vase, in this case a fishbowl, Martha could cross the stems, allowing the flowers to move in every direction. But remember: A dome can be a single blossom in a tiny cup.*

the spiky arrangement *Gladioli (above) are easy to arrange because of their natural height and stiffness. A tall, cylindrical vase holds the stems upright and massed, keeping the big display from spreading out and looking too sparse. The flowers in this arrangement are 'Purple Passion' and 'Pink.' Other spiky candidates—flowers that will naturally shoot upward when placed in a vase—include salvia, delphiniums, foxgloves, flowering branches, and monkshood.* **the single arrangement** *The shape of a flower will tell you if it is dramatic enough to go solo or if it needs to be massed with others. An Oriental poppy (top left) stands alone in the sunlight, revealing its wide, papery petals.* **the floating arrangement** *Bright sunflower faces (left) peer up from individual Fire-King mixing bowls. Martha cuts off the stems and floats the flowers to create an informal centerpiece. Floating them allows you to turn a few flowers into a big arrangement—and is a wonderful way to salvage blossoms with damaged stems. Float as many flowers as you like in one container, depending on the proportions of both the vessel and the blooms.*

the free-form arrangement
*Soft, blowsy roses and peonies
are perfectly offset by cream-
streaked hosta leaves in a
1940s American pottery vase.
Martha wove together the
flowers and used the motion of
variegated foliage to create an
overflowing, cascading effect.
The flowers were cut at various
lengths before being inserted
one by one. The hosta leaves,
which frame and extend the
flower shapes, were added last.*

the grouped arrangement *Martha likes to make numerous small
bouquets that match or complement one another and combine them for
greater impact. Three glass tumblers filled with three colors of roses top
a cake stand for a pretty, light-filled centerpiece. Because they're so
simple, grouped arrangements almost always look spontaneous: Try
making multiple centerpieces in alternating colors to run in a row down
the length of a table, or make bouquets of different sizes—using the
same combination of materials in each—to create a grand still life on a
holiday sideboard. After a dinner party, multiples can be distributed
throughout the house, perhaps on nightstands and bathroom ledges.*

choosing the right vase

Even if you choose the flowers first, the vase is where the arrangement itself starts. And so understanding how to arrange flowers begins with understanding how to look at vases. Just for fun, take a single rose—pink perhaps—and put it in a tall silver bud vase. It's regal, like a woman dressed for church, proud in pastel. Now take the same rose, and cut the stem nearly to nothing. Float the flower in a shallow bowl so that the bottom petals lap the water and the top ones reveal a range of colors that weren't so obvious before.

Neither is better, and both are good. As beautiful as flowers are in the garden, their shapes and sizes need not always dictate how they are arranged once you bring them indoors, but you should respect their inherent beauty. Flowers interact with their surroundings, natural or man-made. The containers that hold them can transform them across their full range of their personalities.

Although the choices might seem overwhelming, most vases fall into six basic categories: the bottle, the cylinder, the sphere, the low pan, the pail, and the trumpet. Look closely. An urn is really just a footed pail. A ginger jar is really a sphere. It makes sense to own at least one contain-

er from each category—or, better yet, several sizes in each. With these six shapes at your disposal, you will never arrive home laden with an armload of sunflowers or with a handful of lilies of the valley, confront all the vases in your cupboard, and decide that nothing, absolutely nothing, is suitable.

But any one shape can lead you in numerous directions. A trumpet, for example, may be petite enough to hold a posy of spring's first crocuses, or it could be as large as an umbrella stand, as dramatically scaled as the gladioli that parade across your flower bed. That trumpet may be made of silver, its finish pleasingly worn, a reminder of the years it spent in your grandmother's home. It may be ceramic or stone. Or, of course, it may be glass, in which case there are special considerations: The stems will become part of the arrangement, so groom them as carefully as the flowers. And as beautiful as glass may be, with light flowing through the vase, the water should be changed every day so it always looks fresh and sparkling, never murky.

The texture of the vase is such a big part of an arrangement, especially one intended for a special event or table setting,

Containers in six basic shapes and various sizes allow you great flexibility in arranging flowers—they hold stems upright, tilt them, let them sprawl, or allow them to float, like this pink water lily in the white low pan. Texture and color, too, affect the impression: the white ceramic vase accentuates the snowy-white apple blossoms that fringe dark branches.

bottle

cylinder

sphere

low pan

pail

trumpet

Most vases are a variation on one of six shapes, illustrated here by a selection of Martha's vases. The bottle is narrow at the top. The sphere, when filled with flowers, creates a lush globe. The pail widens slightly at the top, giving flowers freedom. The cylinder is best at showing off big bunches of flowers. The low pan calls for floating blooms or a glorious spray anchored with a frog: it is the only shape that does not control the stem. The trumpet flares at the top.

that sometimes you will select the vase first, then decide on the flowers. Some floral designers believe that the material and design of the vase should be similar to the flowers in its level of formality and sophistication, like a cut-glass compote filled with old-fashioned peonies. Many, however, prefer to mix things up, using vases and flowers that don't seem to match at all. A vintage sap bucket or weathered clay pot overflowing with refined English roses creates an interesting juxtaposition.

The more you work with flowers, the more likely you'll find a favorite shape, one that allows you the greatest artistic freedom

without sacrificing control. It may be the sphere, with a medium-size opening and large interior that let the stems spread out but keep the flowers from flopping to the sides. Or maybe you'll become devoted to the pail, which some consider the little black dress of the vase world. The trumpet will let flowers flow out more naturally and gracefully extend the shape of the vessel. A vase with a square or rectangular opening can be very easy to work with because the flowers tend to fall in an interesting way on their own accord. Depending on its proportions, the cylinder, with its straight sides, can pose a challenge if it is too constricting,

though a tall, narrow one is usually perfect for tulips because it keeps their reaching, elongating stems under control.

You can work with the nature or habit of a flower to expand its possibilities. A particular flower can be made to behave in many ways, in many containers. In a short cup you can squeeze a dozen lilacs, snipped short, so that their blossoms form one dense mass; or you can arrange them loosely in a tall cylinder, dangling from their spare, gray branches. You can remove all of the foliage from roses or hydrangea, or leave the flashes of contrasting green attached, framing the blooms around the rim of the vase. Remove the buds of calendula or dahlia that may never flower, and you'll give more life to the blooms that remain, altering the flower's presence.

A vase, of course, need not be a "vase" at all. Just about any vessel you have on hand can be pressed into service as a container for cut flowers: beakers, measuring cups, fishbowls, teapots, teacups, pretty bottles, compotes, galvanized flower buckets, pewter bowls, shot glasses, stemmed goblets, watering cans, crystal decanters. Search your garden shed and basement and attic—and tag sales—for inspiration and possible trophies; these places can be treasure troves of useful containers. Martha will often use whiskey and cordial glasses for a little bunch of drooping snowdrops or small clusters of full-blown roses. "I love the way clematis looks floating in a bowl of water," she says. If a container is not watertight or might be damaged by water, simply line it with plastic wrap or set a jar or plastic container inside to hold the water.

Size is another matter. Far too often, people make the mistake of choosing a vase that's much too large for the quantity of flowers they have on hand—their arrangements end up looking skimpy and bedraggled. Unless you are using a low pan, which can be dramatic with a lone flower floating magically in it, select a vase that will allow your flowers to look abundant. Experiment. Try new combinations. Cut the flowers especially short, and be surprised by the effect. Fully opened flowers barely peeking over the top of a container look lush and beg to be embraced—the object of any arrangement.

When choosing between a translucent and opaque vase, consider the effect. Visible in a glass cylinder (above), a modernist twist of calla-lily stems is part of the arrangement; a ceramic vase shifts attention to the blooms. Opaque vases will also hide an arrangement's inner workings, such as a frog or floral tape. Some of Martha's favorite choices for alternative vases (below) include egg cups, fishbowls, teapots, tureens, pitchers, and goblets.

conditioning cut flowers

When you cut a flower from the garden and put it in a vase, it is still a living thing. Even though it is separated from the roots that nourished it in the ground, it still has two essential needs: food and water. By using certain techniques, called conditioning, you can help it get as much of each as possible and keep it looking fresh and healthy far longer than you might expect.

Each type of flower has its own system for conducting food and water through its tissues, so techniques that work for one flower might not be right for another. Florists use a variety of tricks to keep flowers looking fresh, and they're all based on an understanding of the botanical structure of each plant. But you don't need a degree in botany to learn the basics.

If you are buying cut flowers from a shop, you don't have to worry about conditioning them; the florist will have already done it for you. But whenever you pick flowers from your garden or buy a bunch at a farm stand or wholesale flower market, follow these simple steps to keep them in good shape for as long as a week—or more.

When gathering flowers from your garden, it is best to cut them early in the morning, after a cool night has restored their vitality, or just after sunset, when they are filled with food. Necy Fernandes, a contributing editor at MARTHA STEWART LIVING who often cuts and arranges flowers from Martha's garden at Turkey Hill—Martha's Westport, Connecticut, house—generally collects flowers just after sunrise. Avoid cutting in the heat of the day, when flowers are limp and stressed by the sun.

Choose flowers with buds that are tight but that are just beginning to open, unless you need them for a party that night. If you are picking more than a few, be sure to place the cut stems in a bucket filled with tepid water; don't wait until you get back to the house. You want the stems to draw as much water as possible. If you cut a stem and leave it exposed to the air, the cut will begin to heal and seal itself, ultimately causing the flower to wilt.

Once you bring the bucket inside, each stem needs to be cut again. Fill a sink with cool water, and submerge each stem as you recut it. According to Denise Lee, a consultant for the Society of American Florists, if the stems are not cut under water, they will take in air, making it difficult

Cut flowers, like these pink and white ranunculuses and green viburnum blossoms in milk-glass tumblers, can last a week or longer. Florists use simple tricks and techniques, called conditioning, to strengthen and add vitality to flowers before composing arrangements. Supplied with a handful of tools and knowledge, anyone can do the same.

GATHER TOOLS   CUT STEMS   REMOVE FOLIAGE

all flowers	**all green- and woody-stemmed flowers**	**all flowers**
To cut and properly prepare any kind of stem, keep on hand these essential tools: a sharp knife, scissors or garden shears, pruners, and a hammer — useful for fraying thick, woody stems, especially those of early spring's flowering branches.	*Cut stems at a forty-five-degree angle. This keeps stems from sitting flat in the vase and creates a large surface area, so that as much water as possible will be absorbed. Use sharp clippers or shears for woody stems, and sharp scissors or knives for other flowers.*	*After cutting stems, remove any leaves or foliage that would otherwise sit under the water line in the vase. Leaves rot when submerged and will contribute to bacteria and algae in the container, which would shorten the life of the blooms.*

for the flowers to get the water they need.

Cut an inch or so from each stem at a forty-five degree angle, creating a greater surface area and allowing as much water as possible to be absorbed. This also prevents the stems from resting flat on the bottom of the container, interfering with their ability to draw water. Use sharp clippers or pruning shears for woody stems, and very sharp scissors or knives for all other flowers. If you use a dull knife or scissors, you can end up tearing the stems, doing more damage than good.

Next, pull off any foliage that will be under the water line; leaves rot when submerged and will contribute to the formation of bacteria and algae in the vase. Place these stripped stems in a deep container filled almost to the top with water, then add a

commercial flower food or a little sugar. In nature, flowers create their own food, converting sunlight into glucose through the process of photosynthesis. Sugar, or flower foods containing sugar, helps nourish cut flowers when they are brought indoors. Allow the flowers to drink deeply for a few hours, then put them in a cool spot overnight.

Do not place flowers in the refrigerator. According to Rene Van Rems, the director of promotion for the California Cut Flower Commission, today's home refrigerators draw moisture away from plant cells, which will only hasten the flowers' demise. Instead, place flowers in a cool closet, basement, or garage. During the night, they will undergo what florists refer to as the "hardening" process, absorbing water that will make them

HOLLOW WOODY BULBS MILKY

amaryllis, delphiniums, lupines, Queen Anne's lace	**lilacs, dogwood, azaleas, camellias, forsythia, crab apples**	**tulips, daffodils, crocuses, grape hyacinth**	**poppies, euphorbia, hollyhocks, zinnias, sunflowers**

Flowers with hollow stems need to stay full of water. After pouring water into the stem, either plug it with cotton balls or put your finger over the bottom to keep the water in, put the flower in a vase, then remove your finger when stem is under water.

Woody-stemmed flowers, like branches of flowering trees, should be split vertically, about an inch or two up the stem, so more water can be drawn. If the stem is very thick, smash the bottom few inches with a hammer until it is frayed.

When preparing to arrange flowers that grow from bulbs, cut off the firm white portion at the bottom of the stem. If you do not remove this thickened tissue, the flower will have difficulty drawing water up its stem.

Most florists say that if a flower exudes a milky substance from its stem, the stem should be dipped in boiling water for thirty seconds or seared with a match to keep the flower from losing nutrients. It will draw water through the sides of the stem.

stronger, stiffer, and more ready to withstand arranging. This is particularly helpful if you are using a floral frog or when making bouquets that will need to be carried or transported before reaching water again.

Most cut flowers need only minimal conditioning to look their best. A few flowers, however, require special treatment.

Lilacs will last longer if you put them in wood alcohol (available at hardware stores) for an hour, then place them in cold water and leave in a cool spot overnight. Never place lilacs in a metal container, or they will wilt.

Because they release a substance that is harmful to other flowers, daffodils and hyacinths should be conditioned separately for twenty-four hours before combining them with other flowers. Some florists

avoid arranging them with spring-blooming flowers altogether. There is a special flower food (see the Guide) for mixed arrangements that prevents the sap from damaging the other flowers.

The offensive smell of marigolds can be neutralized by mixing a tablespoon of sugar into the water in the vase.

When conditioning euphorbia, put the flowers in their own bucket of cool water; otherwise they will mildew and turn yellow.

Amaryllis stems tend to bend and split after they sit in water for a while. This can be remedied if you trim the stems every day or cut the stems very short initially.

If the petals of sunflowers start to look unsightly, carefully pull them out. What is left—the central seeds surrounded by the

CUT ABOVE NODES

REMOVE STAMEN

REMOVE THORNS

carnations

When conditioning carnations, as well as baby's breath and sweet william, be sure to make your cut just above one of the nodes that run up the flower's stalk. This will allow the stem to more easily draw the water it needs.

lilies

The pollen in the stamens of a lily, if brushed on your clothing or your furniture, will leave a stain. Carefully remove the stamens with a tissue or snip them with manicure scissors before putting the flowers in vases.

roses

If you buy roses from a florist, they probably will have already been shorn of their thorns. At home, it is best to pare them with a sharp knife, working from the top down, because it puts less stress on the stem. Or use a stem stripper (see photograph on page 30.)

small green calyx—will continue to look striking and attractive.

Other tricks and secrets for prolonging the life of flowers accompany the photographs in this chapter.

When it is time to arrange your flowers, you must first select a suitable container (see "Choosing the Right Vase," page 18). Scrub it well, using bleach and water to eliminate any bacteria on the surface. Rinse it thoroughly. Fill the vase with tepid water, and add a commercial flower food. This enhancer, sold by florists, will become one of your most useful tools: It is designed to provide the right proportion of nutrients and substances that block the growth of bacteria. If flower food isn't available, add ordinary sugar for nourishment (add a teaspoon of sugar to a gallon of water) and a

tablet of aspirin, an acidic ingredient that enables the plant to more easily absorb water. Lemon-lime soda also works well, providing sugar and acid (add one part lemon-lime soda to three parts water).

Since most flowers last longer in a cool environment, never place your flowers next to a source of heat, such as a radiator, fireplace, or even a television. The exception is if you want the flowers to open quickly; then place them in full sunlight.

Martha refills her vases every day with water that's cold, not room temperature, because she has found the flowers last longer. She also periodically adds a few ice cubes to vases to give flowers a boost.

If the water in your vase begins to look even a little bit cloudy, pour it all out, and scrub the vase in hot, soapy water. Cloudi-

LIMP BLOOMS	STEMS THAT BEND	WATER FLOW

roses	**tulips**	**tulips**

If flowers look limp, submerge them in a bath of cool water, and cover the stems with a towel. They will absorb water through their pores, helping them plump and revive. To keep them submerged, tie them together and attach an anchor, like fishing weights.

Wrap tulips in brown paper or newspaper, secure with twine or a rubber band, and place them in water overnight to keep them from drooping before you arrange them. This works well with any flowers that have a tendency to sway and fall.

If tulips appear to be failing sooner than expected, try this: Insert a pin through the stem just below the head of the flower, then pull it out. The tiny hole will allow air to escape, expediting the flow of water.

ness is a sign of bacteria, which will kill flowers by interfering with their ability to absorb water and nutrients. Recut all stems, and refill the vase with fresh, clean water. Some experts suggest adding a drop of bleach to the water to kill any remaining bacteria.

Be aware that some plants and flowers are poisonous. Handle them with care. Others may contain sap that can irritate the skin and cause rashes, burns, or blisters. Keep them away from children and pets, and try to handle them, wearing gloves, as little as possible during conditioning. Common poisonous plants include ivy, rue, yew, arum lilies, hellebores, foxgloves, lily of the valley, and monkshood. Primula and euphorbia are two common plants that contain sap that can cause dermatitis. If a plant does irritate the skin or eyes, wash the area thoroughly with clean water. Do not hesitate to seek medical attention; take a piece of the plant and, if possible, its label with you.

Remember that conditioning does not mean preserving. Even when properly prepared and confined to a vase, there's nothing static about flowers. Arrangements ripen and mature. Buds fatten up; blooms open to their fullest, most extravagant forms. Some, like tulips, continue getting taller even after they've been cut. In a container, flowers go through a process that is a shortened version of what they would experience in nature. In both the garden and in the house, flowers eventually fade and turn brown. But witness the evolution of a flower up close, and you will be reminded that its intrinsic beauty is different each day, whether it is breaking into full bloom or starting its final fade.

PROLONGING LIFE

ENHANCE THE WATER

all flowers

For cut flowers to survive, they need sugar for nourishment and an acidic ingredient, like lemon-lime soda or aspirin, which allows the plant to more easily absorb water. A drop of bleach prevents bacteria.

building a sturdy foundation

One of the pleasures of arranging flowers is thinking about the effect you want to create. Often, the most natural arrangement is nothing more than a volume of stems held together by the neck of a vase. But many stems, containers, and styles of arrangement call for a few techniques that, like good magic tricks, should not reveal their secrets to the eye. The tools you will need are really quite minimal: floral snips or pruners, floral tape, floral gum, chicken wire, and floral frogs, which can be found in many sizes and styles.

A frog, which sits at the bottom of a vase to anchor and direct the stems, is your most versatile tool. The earliest known examples of frogs date from the fourteenth century and were used in the Japanese art of flower arrangement, or ikebana. Because this technique required the strategic placement of a few perfect blooms, some kind of holder was absolutely necessary. Early forms were fashioned from iron and included variations on horse bits and cooking tripods; later examples ranged from crabs and turtles to decorative openwork designs and pincushions, or *kenzan*, "needle mountains" in Japanese. Each holding technique produced a particular artistic effect, and the frog itself was often part of the look—clearly visible in the traditional low, flat bowl.

In the West, tools for controlling flowers were relatively rare until the late nineteenth century. Unlike their Japanese counterparts, most Western-style arrangements were made up of copious amounts of flowers that filled their containers and were held in place by their own mass or just a lot of wet sand—a trick frequently employed in nineteenth-century America. Today's frogs are mostly the common wire cage or pincushion varieties, but many new, vintage, and antique styles can be found, some of which are quite collectible.

The shapes and habits of the flowers you're working with will help you decide which tools you need and how the arrangement will actually be constructed. Martha uses relatively simple techniques she has learned from floral designers and stylists, methods that produce stunning arrangements that don't require hours to create.

Martha likes to insert the stems of snapdragons and delphiniums, for instance, into a floral frog until the arrangement is lush and spiky. A floral frog provides sup-

Many arrangements can stand on stems alone; those that cannot require various kinds of hidden, underlying support. The wiry stems of these sweet peas, poppies, Queen Anne's lace, and ferns are held in place by a piece of chicken wire fixed with floral tape over the opening of a tole urn. For more on this and other techniques, see the following pages.

This selection of Martha's most-used frogs (above), dating from the twenties to the present, can be used to hold almost any tricky arrangement in place. The one at the bottom combines the holding power of both a pincushion and a steel cage; the tiny pincushion next to it can hold a single stem upright. Wire, pincushion, steel-cage, glass, and ceramic frogs can still be found for dollars apiece at thrift shops and tag sales; new frogs are available at floral shops. Also among Martha's preferred tools for arranging (above right) are floral tape, spooled floral wire, waterproof floral gum, chicken wire, a stem stripper, scissors, and rubber bands.

port at the base of a vase—and so, of course, at the base of the stems.

Wiry-stemmed flowers such as ranunculus, scabiosa, and sweet peas require support when used in loosely styled arrangements. Without it, their stems would rest against the vase's rim, leaving a hole in the center of the arrangement. Such stems need stronger support, from higher within the container than a frog can provide. Many stems are too soft to insert into a frog anyway. Martha either attaches a piece of chicken wire across the top of a container, or she'll ball up a square-foot piece and set it in the container. Both methods provide a loose scaffolding for an open, more casual arrangement.

Small, delicate flowers, like snowdrops and lily of the valley, need still more support, especially when displayed in a compote or bowl. In such instances, Martha attaches strips of floral tape in a grid pattern across the rim of the container. The grid, which gives you the most control, can be made as open or as tight as needed.

In deeper vases, strong, forthright stems provide their own framework and become

part of the overall floral design. Blooming branches, azaleas, rhododendrons, and hydrangea have woodier stems that look elegant and sculptural when knit together in a translucent container. Hollow-stemmed flowers such as calla lilies, tulips, daffodils, and amaryllis look particularly handsome when given a gentle twist before being inserted into a clear, cylindrical vase.

Another trick Martha likes is to build a large arrangement out of smaller bundles of blossoms such as zinnias, tulips, or roses—bound together with rubber bands, wire, or floral tape. Five bundles of five stems each is far easier to manage than twenty-five individual stems.

Martha always allows flowers and branches to maintain their overall integrity. No matter how small or large an arrangement, freshly cut flowers will look better and last longer if their stems are allowed to behave naturally, rather than being jammed into a piece of floral foam, which can damage stems, inhibit the flow of water, and make an arrangement look stiff. Ultimately, flower arranging requires a light hand and an openness to the unexpected.

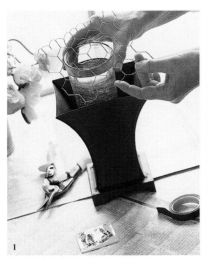 

chicken-wire grid *Without support, the stems in the arrangement on page 29 would have flopped to the side. 1. Martha first placed a glass filled with water in the bottom of the tole urn, which would rust if left in prolonged contact with water. She covered the wide opening with chicken wire cut to fit, and attached it to the urn with pieces of floral tape. 2. She then built the arrangement stem by stem; the fern fronds help obscure the chicken-wire grid.*

floral frog *Snapdragons (far right), by nature, create full arrangements with very little effort. 1. To make this bouquet, you will need a floral frog, waterproof floral gum, and a piece of cellophane large enough to line the glass container to prevent scratches. Martha sticks cellophane to bottom of compote with floral gum. She then affixes more floral gum to the base of the frog and presses it onto the cellophane. 2. To prepare the stems, she removes blossoms and leaves at the bottom. Then, starting in the center, she inserts the stems into the holes of the frog.*

chicken-wire ball *Most floral frogs are too small for certain jobs. With enough support, blooming branches can be easily displayed in shallow containers, like Martha's pressed-glass compote (opposite) and footed bowl (left). 1. Ball up a square-foot piece of chicken wire, and press it in place with four or five pebble-size balls of floral gum. 2. Begin by inserting the tallest branches in the center and adding shorter ones until the chicken wire is hidden.*

floral-tape grid *Small flowers that droop, like snow-drops and lily of the valley (right), often need extra support in wide containers. 1. Attach strips of quarter-inch floral tape one inch apart to the rim of the bowl, creating a grid. A half-inch overhang keeps the tape tight and will not show once the arrangement has been completed. 2. Beginning in the middle of the grid, fill the holes with the tiny lilies and snow-drops. The trick is to envelop each lily of the valley in one of its broad leaves and to cluster each snowdrop with several of its slender leaves. Finish the arrangement off with a ring of snowdrops to cover the tape.*

short flowers, tall vase *Here's a trick to make tall vases more versatile. When arranging flowers whose stems are too short, start by carefully inserting a jelly jar upside down into an opaque vase, which raises the bottom several inches. Place a flower frog on top, anchoring it with floral gum if necessary, and arrange flowers, like these zinnia 'Envy' and bells of Ireland, as you would in a more diminutive vase. This technique is also easier than aiming long stems into the frog at the bottom of a narrow vase, and it keeps you from dropping a heavy metal frog into a fragile vessel.*

bundled stems *Bring order to what can be an unruly job by bundling. A dense bouquet in a wide container is much easier to construct if you gather flowers into small bunches first. Use rubber bands, floral tape, or floral wire to bind each bunch, then build the arrangement, bunch by bunch. Bunches can be cut to slightly different lengths or nestled above or below one another. A dozen bundles of twelve to fifteen zinnias each (above) fill a massive mixing bowl for a late-summer buffet (left). For arrangements in smaller containers, bundle only three or four stems at a time.*

twisted stems *When they're on view in a clear vase, straight stems (opposite) become more shapely and dynamic if they're given a slight twist. First, build the flowers—in this case snapdragons—into a large, well-formed bunch that will ultimately be a snug fit in the vase; use a rubber band to hold the stems if necessary. Trim stem ends to the same length. Grab stems—one hand at the top, the other at the bottom—and gently but firmly twist in opposite directions (above). Holding the spiraled stems in position, carefully work the bouquet into the vase.*

planting a cutting garden

When a flower gardener starts thinking like a vegetable gardener, what results is a cutting garden. As much as any row of beans or trellis of 'Sugar Snap' peas, a cutting garden is about productivity. Unlike a conventional bed, meant to be appreciated as part of the landscape, the payoff of a cutting garden comes when the blooms are picked, brought indoors, and placed in just the right vase. The cutting garden has not just interior-decorating value, but psychological benefit, too. It spares you the torture of having to decide "to cut, or not to cut"— of actually getting up the courage to go at your beautiful garden with a pair of clippers.

Not so long ago, no home worth its boxwood hedges would have been without a cutting garden any more than it would have been without a kitchen garden for fresh food and herbs. Fresh flowers throughout the house were the expected— and there was no supermarket to run to when guests were on the way and the table was, florally speaking, bare.

Even today, with cut flowers sold in malls and train stations and shipped almost anywhere by mail, making room for a plot to cut from will give you the most flowers for your money. The price of a modest bouquet from a florist, about $25, could instead buy seeds for ten prolific annuals, or better yet, five or six dozen seedlings. Instead of a single bouquet that lasts a week or less, the yield could last two months or longer.

The success of a cutting garden depends on the selection of plants, but which of the ones labeled "good for cutting" are for you? Plants suitable for a cutting garden run the gamut—from annuals, perennials, and biennials to shrubs and ornamental grasses. Annuals tend to be the most popular: They are inexpensive, easy to grow, bloom a long time, and respond well to cutting. However, diversity is important if you want to have interesting arrangements, so choose a variety of colors, textures, sizes, and fragrances. Many people plant cutting gardens that peak in July and August, missing out on early- and late-season charmers. More satisfying is the garden that blooms from early spring to frost. Checking when individual varieties bloom will help you develop your plant list.

A perfectly respectable two-hundred-square-foot cutting garden could be made by planting six seedlings in each of two colors of cosmos (white or pink, and the newly

Unlike the rest of the flower garden, a cutting garden is meant for harvesting. In late summer,
Martha's cutting garden at Turkey Hill is at its peak, yielding armloads of blooms for indoor
arrangements, including deep-blue salvia, pale-purple asters, and multicolored zinnias.
At their very best, cutting gardens offer a beautiful variety of material from spring to frost.

Cutting gardens are typically arranged in rows, so it is easy for Martha to shift her old vegetable beds into cut-flower production beds (above, left to right): After tilling, a row marker is used to stretch string to delineate each row. Row markers are simple tools; the one on the left is new, the one on the right is antique. Seedlings are aligned along the string. Martha's gardener helps her tuck pots of perennials and small annual seedlings into the new plot.

popular orange), two zinnias (a multicolored mix plus a single color like chartreuse 'Envy' or vivid 'Scarlet Splendor'), salvia 'Victoria,' annual ageratum, mixed-color snapdragons, calendula, China asters, and scabiosa, along with a few well-branched, small-headed sunflower plants and one or two torch flowers (*Tithonia rotundifolia).* For another $20, a half-dozen each of six kinds of tulips could fill a small part of the same space for spring use.

The classic cutting layout is row by row, like a garden of food crops—corn here, beans there. It was therefore a smooth transition when Martha transformed her old vegetable garden at Turkey Hill into a cutting garden. Though cutting gardens can be solely annuals, and often are, Martha's plan offered more (see pages 40 and 41). Perennials such as delphinium, lavatera, lavender, *Aster frikartii,* and Japanese anemones were on the list, as were bulbs and bulblike plants—Asiatic and Oriental lilies and a row of dahlias. Even the vegetable trellises in one bed were called into cutting-garden duty, serving as supports for sweet peas early in the season.

Conventional wisdom says to place the cutting garden out of the way, since it emphasizes utility rather than design or per-

fect grooming. But it can also be a landscape feature in a backyard garden where there's no place to conceal it. When there is no room for even a small plot, clever gardeners can always tuck a few favorite cutting flowers into various corners used only part time: tulips and daffodils where the peppers and other summer vegetables don't go in until after the last frost; lily bulbs where spinach comes out in late spring; zinnias and marigolds at the ends of vegetable beds; gladiolus corms in any sunny spot, since a dozen fit in a square foot or less. Even half a dozen checkered lilies (*Fritillaria meleagris*) would be welcome in a bud vase in early spring, as would a shot glass full of snowflakes (*Leucojum*). Both are sold in fall with bulbs and take mere inches of soil.

Whichever scale and organizing principle you adhere to, the basics remain the same. Some people think of their interior schemes when choosing cutting-flower colors and stick to safe pastels. Actually, a surprisingly wide range of hues looks good together. Violet played against orange or chartreuse is outstanding, though it may not occur to you when you're plant shopping. Scabiosa is familiar in pastels, but

the dark-purple double form is distinctive.

In the cutting garden, timing is everything. Martha likes to establish a schedule for sowing and transplanting to increase productivity. Simultaneously sow and plant seedlings of several varieties early in the season to encourage staggered blooms. After that, sow in two-week intervals until midsummer. Cosmos, bachelor's buttons, sunflowers, annual rudbeckia, agrostemma, and scabiosa are good plants to try this way.

To establish very early and very late blooms, in some cases beyond the first few frosts, you need to check which plants can handle cool temperatures. Try sweet peas, which can be planted outdoors well before the frost-free date without protection; larkspur varieties such as 'Giant Imperial,' 'Blue Cloud,' and 'Snow Cloud'; calendula; stock; and snapdragons (although they're better as transplants than sown directly). When you resow for late blooms, always count backward from your first frost date, as you do with late vegetables. Be generous with your timing: If the catalog says ninety days until bloom, make it one hundred days from your frost date. Plants grow more slowly when temperatures cool off. Allowing more time

guarantees that you'll have flowers before the heavy frost sets in. Zinnias are classic among long bloomers that do not require successive planting. Other good choices include gomphrena, ageratum, *Celosia* 'Pampas Plume,' bells of Ireland, *Monarda* 'Lombada,' *Asclepias tuberosa* 'Silky Gold,' cleome, *Verbena bonariensis*, marigolds, salvia, and dahlias.

Some plants require cutting back to about a foot after the first flush of blooms. This is especially important for plants that are hurt by heat. Once you've cut them back, fertilize for a second bloom period in the fall (the next flush may not be as tall). Giants like tall cosmos can be hacked back halfway or more in midsummer, and will fill out and bloom all the way to frost after a short break. Other plants that respond well to this treatment are phlox 'Tapestry Mix,' ageratum, lisianthius, rudbeckia, and snapdragons.

Like any garden, the cutting plot thrives on maintenance. The most important task is deadheading—cutting off spent flowers—even if you don't need the blooms for a bouquet. If they're allowed to go to seed, many plants will simply stop putting out fresh crops of flowers. And that would certainly foil the best-laid cutting-garden plan.

Organizing and labeling will help you manage a cutting garden most productively (above, left to right): Perennials and small annual seedlings are laid out before planting; the garden is already bright with edible chive blossoms. Martha prefers to use copper tags to help distinguish each variety—inconspicuous and easy-to-read, they are perfect for recording start dates. Hot-pink zinnias are among the annuals. Aster frikartii is one of the perennials in the plan.

Planting a variety of flowers in similar colors allows Martha to create mixed arrangements whose beauty is enhanced by keeping to a narrow range of colors. Here, Martha finishes an all-lavender arrangement of physostegia, phlox, gomphrena, Verbena bonariensis, zinnias, and salvia.

planning martha's cutting garden

Martha changed her old vegetable garden in Westport, Connecticut, which is enclosed by trellises of climbing roses, into a large-scale cutting garden arranged row by row. Each year she changes the selection of flowers. The first year, it included annuals for both fresh and dried use, as well as some of her favorite perennials and a few bulbs. The white and pink roses, though not technically planted as part of the cutting plan, were fair game. In the illustration on the opposite page, each stripe of color represents a row about two feet wide, with a foot-wide path in between. A few of the plants, such as sunflowers and *Tithonia*, need the space of a double row. Some of the larger cosmos varieties also get quite bushy. They may need more space than a snapdragon or a China aster, and staking, too, so they don't topple. Certain smaller plants, such as the delphiniums, were also staked to keep the flower stems straight. All the others (except flowers to be used dried, such as gomphrena, strawflowers, and statice) were deadheaded regularly to prevent them from going to seed and instead encourage them to produce a continuing harvest of blooms. Flowers to be dried were picked as they reached their peak of color, and were then hung to dry for later use.

Most of the perennials and annuals were planted after the final frost date in midspring, which was May 31 in this case. But as with any gardening project, there was a need for more plants later on to fill in the holes where animals or weather had done their damage. Martha bought a smaller selection of seedlings around the Fourth of July, widening the list and also extending the season a bit, since some of the fresher plants began blooming later and lasted right through the first frost.

Martha's cutting garden, which measures an impressive fifty-five by one hundred and fifty feet, produces a surplus of flowers. Most of us would be well served by having one small and one large arrangement each week through the summer—even a two-hundred-square-foot cutting garden would yield a greater harvest than that. Once you have established a cutting garden or patch and arranged it in a way that allows you to see the flowers as an actual crop, you'll learn that what seemed too perfect to pluck from the main garden can be picked free of guilt.

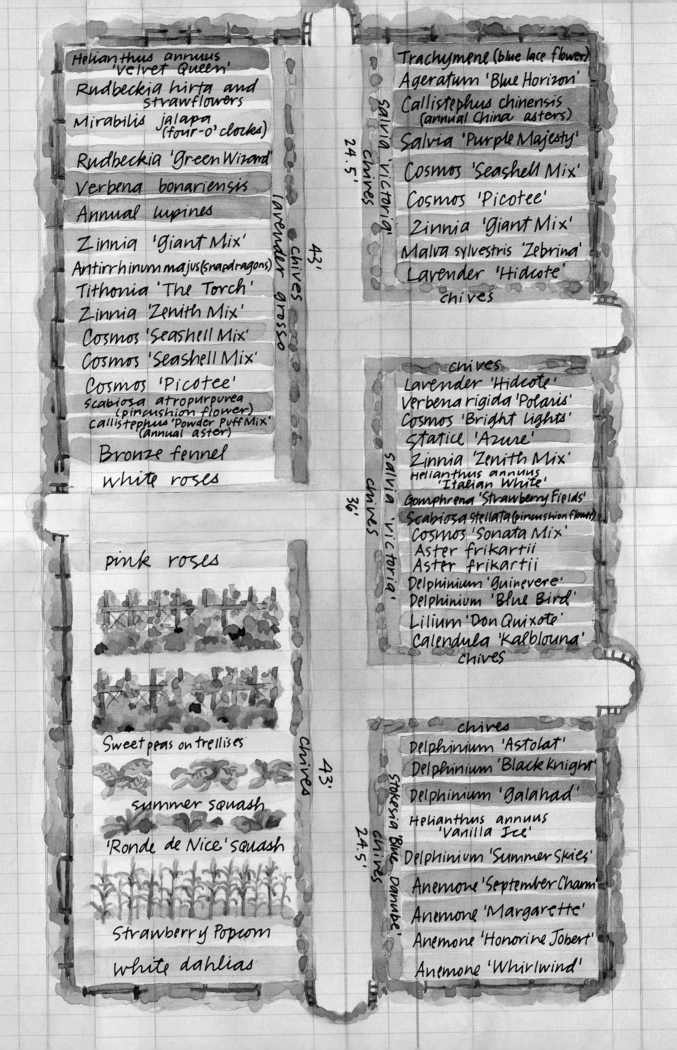

Helianthus annuus 'Velvet Queen'

Rudbeckia hirta and strawflowers

Mirabilis jalapa (four-o'clocks)

Rudbeckia 'Green Wizard'

Verbena bonariensis

Annual lupines

Zinnia 'Giant Mix'

Antirrhinum majus (snapdragons)

Tithonia 'The Torch'

Zinnia 'Zenith Mix'

Cosmos 'Seashell Mix'

Cosmos 'Seashell Mix'

Cosmos 'Picotee'

Scabiosa atropurpurea (pincushion flower)

Callistephus 'Powder Puff Mix' (annual aster)

Bronze fennel

white roses

lavender grosso

chives

24.5'

43'

salvia 'Victoria' chives

Trachymene (blue lace flower)

Ageratum 'Blue Horizon'

Callistephus chinensis (annual China asters)

Salvia 'Purple Majesty'

Cosmos 'Seashell Mix'

Cosmos 'Picotee'

Zinnia 'Giant Mix'

Malva sylvestris 'Zebrina'

Lavender 'Hidcote'

chives

chives

Lavender 'Hidcote'

Verbena rigida 'Polaris'

Cosmos 'Bright Lights'

Statice 'Azure'

Zinnia 'Zenith Mix'

Helianthus annuus 'Italian White'

Gomphrena 'Strawberry Fields'

Scabiosa stellata (pincushion flower)

Cosmos 'Sonata Mix'

Aster frikartii

Aster frikartii

Delphinium 'Guinevere'

Delphinium 'Blue Bird'

Lilium 'Don Quixote'

Calendula 'Kalblouna'

chives

36'

salvia 'Victoria' chives

pink roses

Sweet peas on trellises

summer squash

'Ronde de Nice' squash

Strawberry Popcorn

white dahlias

chives

43'

24.5'

Stokesia 'Blue Danube' chives

chives

Delphinium 'Astolat'

Delphinium 'Black Knight'

Delphinium 'Galahad'

Helianthus annuus 'Vanilla Ice'

Delphinium 'Summer Skies'

Anemone 'September Charm'

Anemone 'Margarette'

Anemone 'Honorine Jobert'

Anemone 'Whirlwind'

One of Martha's favorite ways to display the harvest from her cutting garden is to make a bouquet of various hues of the same variety of flower. Allowed to flop on the ends of their delicate, irregular stems in an unstructured fashion, double-petaled scabiosa blossoms (below) in pink, wine red, and deepest purple invite closer inspection. The narrow-necked container holds the stems snugly in place. Long familiar as an old-fashioned cottage-garden favorite, scabiosa is a profuse bloomer, producing its flowers on tall stems from midsummer until the frost. The cut blooms typically last for a week in arrangements.

For a fall bouquet (top) in brilliant yellow and orange, Martha arranged vibrant bloomers: lantana, calendula, zinnias, and double helianthus. Contrasting colors create an effect all their own: Spiky salvia 'Victoria,' chartreuse zinnia 'Envy,' and a like-colored nicotiana (above) are supported by the foliage of an unknown milkweed a friend collected in Mexico.

Annuals provide the perfect material for casual summer arrangements. A loose bouquet (above) of orange and white cosmos, small white *Zinnia linearis*, white spires of salvia, and melampodium makes an especially refreshing display. A bunch of cool-blue cornflowers (above left) proves there is little as charming as a handful of one type of flower in a simple container. Among the stars of the late-summer cutting garden, marigolds (left) make lasting cut flowers; in the shade beneath the pergola at Turkey Hill, 'Lady's Mix' marigolds fill the top of a strawberry pot, while bunches of little 'Gem Hybrid' marigolds and orange cosmos peek from the sides.

Bouquets
Throughout
the
Year

Four seasons

of arrangements

at Martha's

show that there

is no corner

in a home that

will not benefit

from the presence

of flowers

Spring begins, say meteorologists, when the average daily temperature reaches forty-eight degrees Fahrenheit. Heed the calendar, and spring begins late in March and ends

late in June. But gardeners have long known otherwise: "So long as we can see some plant in the garden starting off vigorously for its annual round of existence," wrote the English gardener Edward Augustus Bowles in his 1914 classic, *My Garden in Spring*, "so long in that spot is spring with us." The great American garden writer Henry Mitchell wrote that "Gardeners think spring is from late February to mid-April."

The flower arrangements on the following pages start with the first blush of spring, and follow the seasons as they unfold at Turkey Hill—Martha's house in Westport, Connecticut—and at her house in East Hampton, New York. Although the arrangements are divided into spring, summer, autumn, and winter, seasons are not really hard-and-fast divisions in the natural world. Bloom times for flowers vary and overlap from one year to the next. The seasons can be as unpredictable as a rare snowfall in May or a lonely crab apple in full bloom during a December warm spell.

But each season has its own charms, and thoughtful selections of flowers from the garden can be arranged in endless combinations of styles and colors. Martha loves to be surrounded by flowers, outdoors and in. All of her gardens produce more than enough for cutting. In East Hampton, she has some three hundred rose bushes that thrive in the seaside climate. In her new gardens on the rocky coast of Maine, she has planted enough delphiniums to fill the house. And for the past three decades, Turkey Hill, located in Zone 6, has been a beautiful—and expanding—laboratory for growing countless varieties of flowers.

Spring is the busiest time of year in any flower garden—and a favorite time for Martha. It is the time of a thousand tasks. Pansies must be transplanted from flats. Early-blooming perennials need to get into the ground. Flowering trees and shrubs must also be planted. At the same time, outdoor cutting material suddenly becomes plentiful: Crocuses, early tulips, daffodils, hyacinths, and lily of the valley are all making their annual appearance. Forsythia and pussy-willow branches are beginning to burst open. Martha knows her beloved roses are not far behind.

As summer approaches, the subtle pastels of spring's blossoms give way to bolder

strokes of color. Soft pinks and delicate yellows are replaced with a commotion of bold blues, deep purples, and fiery oranges. When the garden is in high gear, Martha often limits her indoor arrangements to just one or two kinds of flowers, but lots of them; she sometimes prefers the pure impact of a mass of one type of flower to the busyness of mixed bouquets.

With the approach of fall, hydrangeas, dahlias, asters, and sunflowers transform Martha's gardens into a changing landscape of autumnal textures and colors. Repeat-blooming roses add their romance and heady perfume to the end-of-the-year show, right up to the first hard frost. Sometimes Martha likes to create arrangements without any blossoms at all; she celebrates the unique beauty of stems and branches by allowing them to stand alone in a vase in an entry hall or on a mantel.

While Martha prefers to arrange her own homegrown flowers, she does not always restrict her floral inspiration to the confines of her gardens. She also finds suitable materials from any number of sources, whether a bucketful of zinnias from a local roadside stand or more exotic flowers from

a wholesale flower market. During the winter holidays, for example, Martha depends on materials such as cut amaryllis or roses from the flower market to design lush, festive decorations.

The arrangements you create may be simpler or more extravagant than some of those found here. Use these bouquets as templates, or use them as inspiration: Adapt the size and palette of the arrangement to suit the mix of flowers in your own garden or region. Try out a new vase, or rediscover a forgotten eggcup or teapot. Each and every bunch of flowers will be the freshest and most satisfying reward.

One of the pleasures of arranging materials from the garden is in appreciating each season's bounty—or scarcity. Spring bulbs at Turkey Hill (above) offer some of the year's first cuttings. By late May at Turkey Hill (previous spread), Martha has a surfeit of poppies and Siberian irises. Hydrangeas in East Hampton (left) will take on deeper hues in autumn. By snowfall (below), after the garden has been put to bed, rose hips and evergreens are among the few remaining offerings; the luxury of blossoms must be sought from the flower market.

[spring]

flowering branches

crocuses

violets hyacinths

narcissi

lily of the valley

lilacs tulips

pansies

The last icy patches of snow have vanished. Small bulbs are sending up their sweet blooms, brightening the garden. Wonderfully fragrant flowers—hyacinth, lilac, lily of the valley—are opening to tempt their pollinators, encouraging this season of renewal. Cheer on the unfolding weeks by bringing the blooms indoors. Cut a branch of quince, provide it with water and warmth, and reveal the promise of an entire garden awakening to spring.

With their linear architecture, branches almost arrange themselves in containers large enough to provide balance. A bold early-nineteenth-century silver-lustre jug (right) high-lights the velvety catkins of pussy-willow branches; the opaque container conceals the roots that may sprout as the catkins fade. Buds of Magnolia x 'Elizabeth' and tassels of sugar maple (below) are set on a mantel to raise the pendent blossoms above eye level; three vintage pottery vases keep the grouping loose and free.

forcing branches

To enjoy flowering branches indoors, you don't have to wait for nature: Late January through March is the time to start gathering branches from trees and shrubs for early forcing. Their cold-weather requirements have been satisfied for the season, and their branches are ready. Cut the ends of gathered branches on a slant with a pair of sharp shears; immediately plunge them into a vessel of tepid water. Try apple, cherry, quince, forsythia, spicebush, huckleberry, and other flowering branches (except lilac, which does not respond well to forcing). Select branches with interesting structures that are heavily budded, and prune back those that are unsightly or obstructing sidewalks or pathways. Leave branches bearing larger flowers, like magnolia, outside on their shrubs until the buds are fat and well-developed. And don't forget to try your hand at forcing leaves and catkins, too. Keep the water in the vases clean and fresh during the slow coaxing period, which can take anywhere from a week to more than a month. Be patient. When the buds are swollen, move the branches to a sunny window to perform their miracle.

Pink-frosted apple blossoms are displayed in an early-twentieth-century clear-glass vase that reveals the beauty of the entire length of the branch. To give an arrangement of fruit-tree branches a full, natural shape, first begin by inserting the tallest branch, then work in the shorter ones until the arrangement appears balanced. A small bowl of pink 'Apple Blossom' amaryllis underscores the grandeur of the arrangement; a mirrored plateau reflects sunlight upward through the blossoms.

Greenish-white dogwood blossoms seem to flutter above an oversize white pitcher. The branches, densely interwoven in the pitcher's generous mouth, were pruned to lend an overall upward sweep to the display. Before being arranged, the bottom few inches of each branch are split to increase its ability to draw water. Dogwood is also available in shades of pink.

An armful of pale-pink cherry blossoms exuberantly announces the arrival of the season. The elegant swell of the nineteenth-century blown-glass apothecary jar allows branches of varying lengths to be crisscrossed, forming a full, shapely spring arrangement. Crab apple, mock orange, or currant can be used to create a similar arrangement.

Saucer magnolia blossoms, their stems cut short, float seductively in a parade of glass custard cups, creating an informal centerpiece. Cut the branches when the large furry buds are just about to open into goblet-shaped flowers and fill the air with a fresh, citrusy perfume. To condition the stems of saucer magnolia blooms, scrape with a sharp knife, then sear the ends in a flame, or dip into very hot water for about thirty seconds. For branches, split the ends, and remove the bottom few inches of bark.

A large 1930s mixing bowl (above) holds an explosion of fragrant purple hyacinths. To build the arrangement, follow the bundling technique shown on page 34. Rather than mix purple crocuses, white crocuses, and irises (opposite) in a single vessel, Martha shows off each flower individually, then groups the bouquets into a quintessential spring display.

There is no such thing as having too many daffodils. Ale glasses (right) that Martha found in Peru are filled with handfuls of mixed Narcissus. Arranged stem by stem, starting with the shortest at the perimeter and gradually getting taller toward the center, an arrangement in a vintage vase (below) features 'Passionale' daffodils; a pincushion frog helps keep the tallest stems stand upright. Miniature Narcissus cut short and tucked into an eggcup (opposite) make a charming addition to a breakfast tray.

understanding narcissus

The daffodil, for many, is spring itself. The botanical term *Narcissus* refers to the genus of flowers with long, flat, hollow leaves that includes daffodils, jonquils, and narcissi. But, in fact, these names are not interchangeable. Daffodils and jonquils are mainly golden with large trumpets; narcissi usually bear clusters of fragrant white or yellow flowers. All daffodils are narcissi, but not all narcissi are daffodils. This genus, however, is more than just yellow and white—the flowers can display pink, orange, red, green, or a combination. There are even double-flowered varieties, which do not form a distinct cup but have a somewhat rumpled effect. Like other spring-flowering bulbs, *Narcissus* requires a cold period for dormancy. Many varieties naturalize readily: If spaced properly and fertilized regularly, bulbs will multiply and not require division for years. By planting combinations of *Narcissus* varieties, blossoms can be harvested for about two months. Deer, squirrels, mice, chipmunks, and most bugs will not eat *Narcissus* since it's poisonous. The key to success is benign neglect: After flowering is over, resist the temptation to tidy up or cut off the foliage. These leaves are working hard, feeding the underground bulbs and preparing next year's flowers.

To make this sunny dome of daffodils, begin with three large blooms held in the crook of your hand. Add flowers, circling the center, to form a globelike cluster. Before inserting bouquet into a vase, cut the stems as evenly as possible, and give them a slight twist (see page 34). A clear jar reveals the swirl of green stems—a perfect foil for the yellow flowers.

Narcissus, in a diversity of shapes and colors in the April garden at Turkey Hill (left), are plentiful enough to make many spring bouquets. Because daffodils exude a substance that's harmful to other flowers, they are best kept to themselves. If you do want to arrange daffodils with other flowers, place them in a container of water overnight before combining them. If time does not allow, dip the cut ends of daffodils in a diluted bleach solution before arranging. The other great spring flower that lends itself to massing is the tulip. This perfect dome of five dozen white tulips (above) is a variation of the arrangement on the opposite page. To make a bouquet of this size, have someone help you: One person holds the bouquet with two hands while the other adds the flowers. Or make a smaller arrangement yourself in a size you can hold in one hand. See more tulips on the following pages.

planning tulips

Tall varieties may appear somewhat stiff in the garden, but indoors, tulips have a grace and presence irreplaceable in springtime bouquets. To have a steady supply for arranging, Martha grows tulips that bloom from April through May in the cutting garden, planting them in slightly raised rows to provide good drainage. Plan for good color combinations, such as yellow and pink; coordinate the bloom times; and plant more bulbs every season to keep your floral factory at peak production. (Most tulips don't perennialize well, so be sure to buy perennial types, and plant the bulbs extra deep.) Cut tulips early in the morning while they are in tight bud. Since tulips with the straightest stems are the easiest to arrange, straighten curved stems; roll flowers inside a sheet of newspaper, plunge the bunch into cool water, allow the tulips to straighten overnight, then remove the newspaper. Tulips droop, so either pack them tightly, or give them room to move in a bigger vase. Tulips will continue to reach for sunlight, and the stems elongate after being cut, so rotate the arrangement regularly. Shorter botanical tulips may also be dug, bulb and all, from the soil and placed in flats to create small indoor gardens.

There are more varieties of tulips to choose from than ever before, from stocky doubles to the wonderfully fringed parrots and the lean and long-stemmed French tulips. Peach-colored tulips (right) preside over a dramatic springtime display that includes two small glasses of white tulips cut unusually short and an assortment of Easter eggs. The stems of several varieties of yellow tulips (above) vary in length; they are held in place with a "frog" of crumpled chicken wire. Short-cropped yellow and white tulips (opposite) placed in a wrought-iron urn are punctuated with clusters of grape hyacinth. The density of blooms and stems alone holds this arrangement in place.

There is no rule for how long a tulip stem should be. In a bouquet dedicated to their blossoms (this page), tulips are cut short. Two contrasting varieties—lily-flowered tulips and the softer Rembrandt tulips—are used to take advantage of their tendency to bend as they age. Arrange thirty of the former in your hand, cut stems, and transfer to a bowl; space six of the latter evenly throughout. Clean white tulips (opposite) spill from an agateware wash pitcher.

Unusual vessels with numerous small openings provide an inventive way to showcase very small flowers in a very big way. Martha's antique Paris-porcelain egg server is an especially pretty—and useful—container for lily of the valley: it can hold enough blossoms to fill the entry hall at Turkey Hill with their intense perfume. Small bunches of the delicate-stemmed flowers are cradled in several leaves and inserted into the server's ring of holes (opposite, bottom); more flowers and leaves fill the center cavity, originally used to hold sauce.

cultivating lily of the valley

Almost any small-flowering bulb can be brought indoors for an early display. Lily-of-the-valley roots, called pips, can be dug up in late winter, potted up in containers, and gently forced inside a warm house to flower weeks ahead of the ones left outside. Not only does lily of the valley produce the loveliest-scented tiny white flowers in late spring, it will do so in the densest of shade. And if you love pink, there is even a flushed-rose variety. Prechilled, potted pips are available at garden centers, nurseries, and through mail-order sources (see the Guide). Planting lily of the valley in spots of varying sunlight throughout the garden will prolong the harvest of cut stems. Don't forget to cut the foliage, too—the sturdy green leaves make a nice addition to delicate arrangements, providing backdrop, balance, and support to the bell-shaped flowers. A small bouquet is lovely in the bedroom, and tiny containers of lily of the valley make appealing place settings for a springtime luncheon: Try using mint-julep cups, little candy jars, or eggcups. The cut flowers will stay fresh and white for four or five days in a warm room.

Eggshells set in simple eggcups (top) are joyous bud vases for a springtime table. Make a hole in the top of each egg with a pin; enlarge holes to desired size, and pour out the insides. Carefully rinse shells; then, if desired, dye with food coloring (follow package instructions). Juice glasses, too, make sweet bud vases. Cut with a grape motif (above), these hold clusters of Muscari, or grape hyacinth, on a table set for tea.

A cast-iron urn (right) lifts a colorful mix of pansies above the garden floor, the better to be enjoyed during a stroll at Turkey Hill. When arranging pansies, remember that their short, weak stems should be gently placed in small, low containers. Martha's 1920s milk-glass tumblers (below) are just right.

reviving violets

Shy and unassuming, violets and their relatives—pansies, violas, and Johnny-jump-ups—hide their faces among their heart-shaped leaves close to the cool ground. If picked or deadheaded regularly, many violets will continue to flower through the summer and into the fall. Gathered from the spring garden when they are plentiful, violets make worthy ingredients for little bouquets. Some violets are celebrated for their perfume. A sweet-scented violet, *Viola odorata*, has become the deep-purple delicacy of the cut-flower and perfume industries. Violets absorb water through their petals and leaves, so keep them well-misted to look their best. To revive a bunch of wilting violets, plunge them into cold water, blossom and all, for half an hour, then wrap them in a damp paper towel, and refrigerate for two to three hours before arranging.

In a trumpet-shaped wine goblet, a small posy of unusual black pansies with yellow eyes (Viola x wittrockiana 'Black Prince') has a striking presence. Pansies bloom in an ever-growing profusion of single colors, bicolors, and tricolors that include white, yellow, cream, peach, mahogany, red, purple, orange, pink, lavender, blue, and maroon.

It's hard to imagine a display of flowers more innocently delightful than this pair of petite pansy bouquets (above). The lemon-yellow and blood-orange flowers burst from two-inch-tall footed eggcups from France. Such tiny arrangements make endearing place markers for a weekend brunch or shower. Flowers with almost no stems can be gently balanced around the rim of a pansy ring, like this old-fashioned English heart-shaped one (right) of frosted green glass. Pansy rings, which are more often round or oval, can be filled with many other types of flowers, like zinnias and gladioli, if the stems are cut very short (see page 109). Weak-stemmed flowers will support one another if gathered into a dense bunch. Before being set in a 1930s Glidden McBean ceramic tumbler recruited from Martha's kitchen (opposite), this lush bouquet of violets in shades of purple gets a vibrant lift from a single yellow flower tucked into the side.

This armload of classic
American lilacs, massed one
stem at a time in an antique
fishbowl, could perfume a space
the size of a ballroom. The
generous globe lets the lilacs
sprawl in all directions, creating
a profuse, frothy display. Many
of the leaves were stripped
off the branches, but some
were left intact for contrast.

Cut lilacs in full bloom for a bouquet, and you will have begun to prune the lilac tree. In fact, it's wise to prune all the flowers before they fade, because the large seedpods that lilacs form will sap energy from the plant. To keep her lilac trees in top condition, Martha prunes remaining flowers off just as they finish. Only a misshapen or overgrown plant would require harsher pruning. But don't prune after July 4: At that point, lilacs begin setting next year's flower buds, and all you'll be doing is thinning or eliminating next year's display.

Sweet-smelling, blowsy lilacs are not averse to a bit of tailoring. Stripped of their heart-shaped leaves, these individual stems of lilac were crisscrossed, one by one, in a 1930s blown-glass water goblet to form a perfectly formal crown. Lilac florets—the tiny flowers that make up the larger clustered flower heads—may be single, with one row of petals, or double, and vary in size and shape, as do the clusters. Lilacs come in seven colors: white, violet, blue, lavender, pink, magenta, and purple, with many shades of each. Lilacs will be healthier, and arrangements will last up to a week, if the stems are plunged into water as soon as possible after they've been cut from the tree. But don't use a metal container, or the flowers will wilt.

[summer]

snapdragons

sweet peas

gladioli peonies

lilies zinnias

poppies

roses irises

alliums

Longer days and strong sunlight are coaxing grander flowers and ever more color from the garden. Peonies are unfurling their heavy blooms, asking to be cupped by a passing hand. What was so hopefully planted in spring is now offering vibrant rewards. Never is there more to choose from. Chances are a handful of flowers for a modest bouquet won't be missed from your garden. And roadside stands always beckon with an extra bunch or two.

A vintage tole apple basket
makes a lighthearted container
for pink peonies framed by
hosta leaves. Since the metal
basket could rust or leak,
water-filled jars inside hold the
peonies in place. Although
built one stem at a time, this is
a quick and casual arrangement.
Tuck in the hosta leaves last.

cutting peonies

In early June, when her peonies are blooming and summer is making itself known, Martha likes to entertain. Thirty or more varieties of peonies grow everywhere in her Connecticut garden—there are so many flowers that she cuts hundreds for display all over the house. Peonies can make long-lasting arrangements: If cut as just-opening buds, they will gradually unfurl their petals over a ten-day period. Peony plants grow to about three feet tall and have nicely textured leaves that remain attractive throughout the growing season. The slightly perfumed flowers, which can reach five inches in diameter, can be white, cream, pink, red, lavender, rose, coral, or yellow. The full, plump, double-flowered varieties are the most popular, but there are also single, anemone, and semi-double-flowered peonies, as well as Japanese peonies with a single row of large petals. Because the double-flowered varieties produce heavy flowers requiring support, a wire peony ring is indispensable; be sure to put it in place over the plant when the first red shoots appear in early spring. To encourage larger flowers, remove side buds and allow just the main bud to bloom. If it looks like it is going to rain, cut any peonies in full bloom, since dampness will shorten their life.

There is no grander old-fashioned flower than the double pink peony. Combined with chartreuse lady's mantle blossoms and small clusters of pink phlox (left), it makes a pretty centerpiece with lots of ruffles. Lay a grid of floral tape (see page 33) over a compote; then insert the peonies, starting on the outside and building around and upward to achieve a nicely rounded dome. Tuck clusters of phlox and lady's mantle into the open spaces. Big tree-peony blossoms (above) look grand when arrayed individually in teacups.

Peony blossoms always seem luxurious and extravagant. Why not create an arrangement that does them justice, and cut them full-blown? Amethyst-glass tumblers (above) support a row of large tree peonies for a garden-party decoration. Several dozen double white peonies with red centers (right), held in place with a floral frog in a pressed-glass compote, are especially elegant with some of their handsome dark-green leaves intact. A grand show, however, doesn't always demand a multitude of flowers: Only five open peonies (opposite) float in a mid-nineteenth-century English transferware punch bowl in Martha's Turkey Hill dining room. Cut the stems to less than an inch before setting in water; if a flower has trouble floating, use a flower float or improvise: Cut a circle of Bubble Wrap, leaving a ring of bubbles intact, and thread the stem through the center bubble.

The profusion of Martha's summer garden is represented in the fireworks of a grand display (right), including lilies, delphiniums, and astilbe. Cut short, large, trumpet-shaped lilies make excellent "knitters," pulling together diverse elements and helping opposites attract. 'Stargazer' lilies (opposite) work their magic when combined in a late-summer bouquet of porcelain berries and double pink Japanese anemones. The ornate Spode pedestal vase was acquired at an antiques store in New York City.

The drama of this photo (left) is deceptive—the arrangement is actually quite dainty, perfect for a bedside table. Start with a wine goblet. Gather a bunch of lilies—the ones used here are the popular and widely available Asiatic hybrids, a short flower with a bloom that faces up—and place them in the center. Then arrange some informal pink snapdragons so they follow the gentle curves of the lilies' petals, like lovely green and pink shadows. Plant snapdragons for harvesting before and after summer's greatest heat, when the flowers would languish. Lilies and snapdragons come in so many colors—use them to create wonderful combinations.

Flowers that grow on tall stalks can be difficult to mix with other blooms, so Martha usually arranges them on their own. The stems of these pink and white foxgloves have been stripped of their leaves, then arranged like a tepee and twisted slightly to support the reaching flowers above. The 'Excelsior' hybrid series of the familiar foxglove (Digitalis purpurea) holds its flowers straight out from its stalk, not pointed toward the ground. It is the longest-lasting of all the foxgloves for cutting.

Keeping the type and color of flower constant lends serenity to any large arrangement. Here, cool-blue delphiniums burst from a clear-glass vase. The stems were cut at various lengths to take advantage of the container's shape; the lowest stalks, inserted last, extend only a few inches into the water. The irregular stems in the vase mirror the spikiness above.

The bearded iris is a distinctive and regal perennial that comes in colors as diverse as a rainbow, which is precisely why they were named for Iris, the Greek goddess of the rainbow. Cut short, iris blooms (left) flow over one another and spill from the sides of a lustreware cup. The colors and textures of the petals beautifully complement the amethyst pressed-glass dessert plates.

The delicately veined and ruffled petals of irises are wonderful to observe in a sunlit window. A single iris or a handful enliven any windowsill. Here, richly colored bearded irises (right) are cut short enough that their blooms cascade seductively over the edge of an antique wine rinser. Candles may be the familiar beacons in an entryway, but two trumpet vases (opposite) filled with Martha's deep-violet beardless Siberian irises are just as welcoming. The stems were cut so that the blossoms in each vase reach between one and three inches above the rim. Long-stemmed irises last anywhere from two to six days in cut arrangements.

Just a few starry alliums cut very short make dreamy bedside companions; these three hover above little glasses on a turn-of-the-century pressed-glass dresser tray. The arrangement is softened by a pale chartreuse linen tablecloth, folded in thirds and used as a runner. Alliums make great cut flowers, and though they are members of the onion family, few give off a significant odor. If necessary, change the water regularly to minimize any unpleasant aroma.

"Alliums are totally modern and totally old-fashioned at the same time," says Martha.
'Globemaster' (largest purple, foreground), 'Mount Everest' (two whites), Allium karataviense
(silvery pink, lower left), and the close allium cousin Nectaroscordum siculum, formerly labeled
as an allium (the tassel-like flowers, top and left), are among the harvest in Martha's garden.

In Martha's Westport garden
in May (opposite), floating
pom-poms of 'Globemaster'
and Allium giganteum compete
with the spires of foxtail lilies
(Eremus) for attention, above
all the daisies and poppies.
From the same garden, five
Oriental poppies (this page),
leaning from etched flip glasses,
form a breezy centerpiece.
The flowers encircle a fancy
wheel-cut apothecary bottle atop
an antique mirrored plateau.

An Iceland poppy (opposite, center right) is surrounded by both named varieties and unnamed seedlings of Oriental poppies from Martha's garden. The deeply fringed cultivar is 'Curlilocks,' the large scarlet one at upper right is 'Carmine,' and 'Cedar Hill' is at lower left. A profusion of Iceland poppies (this page), mostly in pastel shades, reaches and winds in a simple yet elegant table arrangement. The stems are held in a wire frog.

A feast of large, red Oriental poppies (below) brightens the countertop in Martha's Westport kitchen. The papery flowers are arranged in a large vintage wire frog set in an 1870s English transferware tureen. An assortment of Oriental poppy blooms and buds (right) is arranged in a more unstructured style — without a frog — in a crystal celery vase. Oriental poppies come in white, scarlet, orange, pink, and peach; their cup-shaped blossoms are short-lived indoors, lasting two to four days.

conditioning poppies

Fully opened poppies wilt quickly once cut. If the stems of buds have been seared, however, their crinkly tissue-paper petals will slowly emerge for a series of new flowers for up to two weeks. Dip a stem in boiling water for twenty to thirty seconds, or sear it with a flame from a match, gas stove, or butane lighter to keep the flower from wilting and to give it a longer life. The flowers will subsequently drink water through the sides of their stems. Even after the petals fall, poppy stamens persist for a dramatic table arrangement. There are just four species of poppies that contribute to the spectacle of color in the garden. The only perennial species of importance, the Oriental poppy, is usually planted in late summer, when its roots are dormant. The Opium poppy (which is illegal to grow in the United States) and the corn, or Flanders, poppy are annuals from Europe. The Iceland poppy is an unreliable perennial best treated as an annual. Poppy seeds can be scattered where you hope they will grow, but the dabs of impressionistic color that poppies give the garden will not be exactly where you expected them.

Martha's antique Royal Doulton bowl is a lovely container for these creamy-white ranunculuses. A frog was secured in the bowl with floral clay; then, starting in the center, the stems were inserted until a relaxed dome took shape. Smaller blooms and unopened buds rise from and trail lazily over the sides, adding variety to the scale of the flowers.

At Turkey Hill (opposite),
a gate inspired by one Thomas
Jefferson designed for Monticello
is flanked by a profusion of
pink climbing roses, inviting
visitors to explore the garden
beyond. That same sense of
abundance is carried indoors
in Martha's bedroom in East
Hampton (this page) with
an armful of garden roses in
a tight range of soft colors.
Big pink antique 'Comte de
Chambord' roses and the modern
apricot-colored 'Abraham
Darby' are combined into an
arching dome in a nineteenth-
century blown-glass compote.
The stems were steadied
one by one in a wire frog.

To make an overflowing bouquet of old-fashioned roses (this page), Martha began with the shortest stems and continued adding flowers, letting them rest on those below; tight buds and foliage add depth and texture. A similarly voluptuous bouquet of white roses (opposite) is part of a dazzling grouping with two smaller bouquets and pieces from Martha's prized collection of Victorian mercury glass. The roses include 'Sombreuil' and 'Mme. Zoetmans.'

Reducing a rose's stem length shifts the focus to the blossom itself, emphasizing its supple texture. If your supply of blooms is limited, cut a handful of roses in different colors and sizes, and place them individually in tumblers and stemmed glasses (above); admire them on a sunny windowsill, or group them into a spontaneous, colorful centerpiece. When snipping flowers short for a massed arrangement, adhering to a single color can have its own exquisite rewards. White roses (right) nestle seductively in a 1930s pressed-glass McKee mixing bowl; the blossoms have been packed snugly, so they don't require any kind of hidden support. The unopened rosebuds were added as a final touch to punctuate the display.

Climbing tea roses are clustered in a glazed 1940s container divided into three separate globes: a bit of foliage adds contrast. Commercial roses often won't open their petals this fully, but you can make store-bought roses look more like they came from the garden by selecting ones with plump heads and gently pulling out the petals in the very center to reveal the stamens. Encourage stubborn blossoms to open by cupping them in your palm and then gently blowing into their tight centers; tease open the petals with your finger-tips. After several days, recut the stems — keeping them under water — and rearrange.

A turn-of-the-century carnival-glass fruit bowl holds a bouquet of pastel roses culled from Martha's garden, at once cradling the blossoms and letting them sprawl. The colors and forms of both flowers and container are in cheerful harmony. Open roses have the heft to support one another in the wide mouth of a bowl: keep adding stems until the arrangement looks full and secure. Alternatively, you may wish to bundle three to five stems at a time, building the arrangement as you go (see page 34).

Martha enjoys the drama of
a tiered arrangement. This
Victorian blown-glass epergne,
once used for candy, now holds
a remarkable collection of
garden roses. The flowers on
the bottom tier are cut short
and packed tightly enough to
keep one another in place.

Certain flowers blend remarkably well with others in the garden as well as in arrangements. The pale-yellow flower clusters of lady's mantle are an excellent example. Combined with dusty-peach roses (left) and waxy orange clusters of butterfly weed in a celery vase, lady's mantle lends an open, lacy look to the bouquet. It can also act as more than filler: As floral underpinning (below), it supports and highlights a cloud of white roses in an antique blown-glass fishbowl.

prolonging roses

Those without a garden from which to harvest roses must often rely on a florist—or on the generosity of rose gardeners. To determine the freshness of roses from a florist shop or Greenmarket, press the stems tenderly at their base. They should be firm to the touch. Roses from a florist will have already been conditioned, but those from a Greenmarket or wholesaler will not. It's essential to condition roses as soon as possible. Trim the bottom two inches of each stem at a sharp angle—keeping the stem under water if possible—to increase the area of pithy surface being exposed to water. Wrap the stems in paper, and stand them in a bucket of cool water to which flower food has been added; let them rest for a couple of hours. This will ensure that the blossom heads do not droop. Prolong fading blooms by removing spent petals from around the outside of the flower head. Frequent recutting of stems will further prolong an arrangement. If you're picking roses from the garden, cut the stem just above a five- or seven-leaflet leaf—instead of a three—or that stem may fail to bloom the following year.

Overblown pink English roses (left) are understated and elegant, bursting from the top of a clear-glass tumbler, with more than a hint of their contrasting leaves peeking out. The rich pastels of nostalgic English roses (opposite) complement one another effortlessly and fill the room with sweet fragrance. Large, multipetaled flowers of certain varieties do not allow for tight clustering of the luxurious heads in bouquets. Instead, allow room for the fat blossoms to slowly open. If you want to further integrate the colors, don't remove all of the foliage.

Including shiny dark-green foliage (right) dresses up as well as loosens up rose arrangements. Differences in color, size, and shape provide interest and texture, as do the spiky rosebuds that surround these small knots of red, pink, and white roses. To decorate a table, make a group of similar, but not exactly matching, arrangements.

Sweet peas make gorgeous cut arrangements. These fluffy pink blooms have the same
delicate nature as the 1920s Japanese silver-lustre teapot. Since they are rarely available
for purchase as cut flowers, sweet peas are a sign of a gardener's skills. Martha
prefers the old-fashioned varieties, for they are the ones with the strongest fragrance.

One of Martha's favorite
flowers in a favorite vase:
Pale-pink sweet peas were first
arranged stem by stem in the
hand to form an orderly,
domed bouquet. Martha then
snipped the stems to the same
length and gently slid the
bouquet into an especially tall,
elegant trumpet vase, allowing
the arrangement to spread
loosely. Harvest sweet peas
when it's cool outside; place
them immediately in cold water.

The magnificent blue, pink, or white blossoms
of hydrangeas have an old-fashioned appeal
rivaled by few other summer and autumn
flowers. A handful (above) from Martha's
East Hampton garden (opposite) lounges on
the edge of a bowl; the coarse, dark leaves
heighten the flowers' texture and whiteness.
A deep-purple blossom (right) makes a
wonderful surprise hung from a friend's door.
To make a hanging bouquet, hammer holes
in the sides of an antique cocoa or food tin;
thread ribbon through the holes for a handle,
and knot it on the inside or outside of the tin.
Cut hydrangeas will look fresh for a week
or longer if conditioned properly: Cut them
early in the morning or late in the afternoon.
Immerse the end of each stem in boiling water
for thirty seconds; avoid letting steam wilt
the flower heads. Next, plunge flowers up to
their necks in cold water, and drape paper
towels across the blossoms. Tuck towels into the
container, and mist. Let the flowers rest for
four hours; keep the towels damp by remisting.

Gladioli are easy to arrange because of their natural stiffness. Surrounded by neon-bright dahlias, small-flowered red-yellow pixiola "glads" (right) are anything but shy in an opalescent Depression-glass vase. A fan-shaped vase of the magenta and red gladioli 'Jeannie Rose' and 'Dapper Dan' (below) emphasizes the formality associated with this regal flower. A pink arrangement in a 1930s McCoy olive-oil jar (opposite) is well-suited to the relaxed atmosphere of the terrace at Turkey Hill.

growing gladioli

No other flower has the gladiolus's dramatic presence in arrangements, its impossible petticoat of flouncy blooms against such a resolutely upright stalk. And for all their Victorian charm, gladioli come in a range of subtle colors that are sophisticated and modern, including melon, pistachio, plum, mauve, tangerine, and bisque. Though she does not include a single one in her borders, Martha would not consider her cutting garden a success without a harvest of gladioli to arrange in her collection of vintage pottery. The Latin term *Gladiolus* is the diminutive form of the word *gladius*, meaning "small sword," a reference to its spiky leaves—the visual tip-off that the gladiolus is in the iris family. The gladiolus began life as a genus of wildflowers, mostly from South Africa, with delicate blossoms. The first were brought to Europe by the late seventeenth century, but it wasn't until the 1820s that hybrids began to appear. Gladioli are easy to grow. Martha staggers planting and buys early, midseason, and late varieties— though not the giant ones, which are best left to the flower show or altar—for cut stems late summer through fall. Planting begins in her Westport garden in April and continues about every two weeks until July.

Chartreuse can be hard to wear or to live with in large doses in the home, but in arrangements it looks pleasing and fresh. Martha uses chartreuse with abandon and confidence in the garden. A highly variable color, the only constant is that it contains green and yellow. The big globe of an antique blown-glass fishbowl (opposite) provides balance to a lush cloud of golden-green lady's mantle, plumes of astilbe and filipendula, silvery artemisia, and zinnias. Crosshatch the first several stems to provide a framework, and continue weaving in flowers to make a remarkably secure bouquet. The stems that don't reach to the bottom of the container add a dancing quality. A walk through the garden led Martha to create a subtle combination (right) of three forms and textures in a vintage ceramic pansy ring. See below for how to construct it.

For the chartreuse centerpiece in the pansy ring shown above, Martha gathered green 'Envy' zinnias, 'Green Lake' gladioli, and the heart-shaped leaves of sweet-potato vine 'Margarite.' To make the arrangement, first insert several sweet-potato leaves, their stems cut to an inch or two, into a pansy ring, then tuck in several zinnias and gladiolus blooms, alternating the two flowers. Continue adding leaves and flowers until the circle is complete. Remember to cut the zinnia stems short enough to rest within the ring; cut the gladiolus blooms from the stalk, as close to it as possible. This is a great way to use gladioli—which are usually so dramatic—in a sweet, modest centerpiece.

Zinnias are about as summery and unabashedly cheerful as garden flowers get. Arranged in three brightly colored mixing bowls, these are right at home in the kitchen or decorating a picnic table. You'll have more control over the stems if you bundle several at a time (see page 34), then fill the bowl.

choosing snapdragons

Children have always known that squeezing the sides of the snapdragon's jaw opens the mouth so it can snap closed on an unsuspecting fingertip. But the snapdragon's mouth serves nature, not just curious children: Rather than give its nectar away to just anyone, the snapdragon has adapted itself so that only the correct pollinators can get inside. A large bee, for instance, is heavy enough to open a snapdragon by landing on its lower lip. Although its name sounds fierce, few flowers are friendlier in the garden, providing a distinctive fragrance, wide color range, and strong stems that make them ideal for cutting. If deadheaded regularly, the narrow, dark-green leaves of the snapdragon give rise to tall flowering stalks from early summer to fall. They arrive in a commotion of colors: light pink, dark crimson, deep to faint yellows and oranges, white, and bicolors. There are single flowers and doubles, dwarfs (a foot or less), intermediate (one to two feet), and tall (two to three feet). Snapdragons may react to the intense heat of high summer by taking a break after the first blooming. If so, cut off the flower stalks, and wait for them to rejuvenate in late summer and early autumn. In areas with hot summers, choose a series like 'Rocket,' bred for heat resistance, and stake them well.

A pair of slender blown-glass vases (top) highlights the beauty of both blooms and stems of white and yellow snapdragons: the stems were neatly groomed of their foliage and lower, fully opened flowers. A trio of hot colors (above) forms a dense, flamboyant combination in a trumpet-shaped yellow ceramic vase, while shades of green (left) in a simple arrangement make white snapdragons appear even whiter.

[autumn]

chrysanthemums

hydrangeas

monkshood

dahlias

sunflowers

amaranthus

sedum

What could be bolder than this season's blooms? Many have waited only until now to appear—and many will continue to fill arrangements until the first frost. The final flush of summer and the ripening of fall bring deeper hues—fiery-hot orange, rich purple, warm russet—and dramatic flower shapes. Sedum, now a deep coral, is the perfect match for sunflowers and hydrangea. Harvest the rest of the garden before the last leaf falls.

Don't think of September as
the end of the flower garden—
some of the most vibrant
bloomers make their appearance
now and can last until frost.
Hydrangeas are still flowering
and are deepening in color, and
dahlias, those gutsy saviors in
any garden past its seasonal
prime, have arrived. Here, in
showy colors, they are massed
in a fishbowl; Martha placed
the metal frog on folded
plastic wrap (opposite, bottom)
so it won't scratch the glass.

overwintering dahlias

For cutting, the dahlia is a delight, lasting from five to seven days in a vase and producing its flowers from late summer through fall, when many other plants have given up. Since there are thousands of varieties in the trade—and many times that in official listings—virtually any color can be had. The American Dahlia Society recognizes an astounding seventeen distinct shape categories, resembling everything from pinwheels to pom-poms, from less than two inches wide to more than seventeen. Besides white, there are yellows from pale to acid, all shades of red from fire engine to velvety maroon, and orange to bronze. Dahlias come in all manner of pinks, from screaming neon to lavender to purple, as well as startling bicolors and variegates that in their hottest combinations look more tie-dyed than botanical. In cold-winter parts of the country, it is necessary to dig up dahlia tubers after the first frost; place them in a single layer in a newspaper-lined box, and cover with perlite, dry sand, peat moss, vermiculite, or sawdust. Store in a cool (around forty degrees), dry, dark place until replanting in spring. Check occasionally, and lightly moisten if necessary.

"The Dahlia's first duty in life," wrote the English gardener Gertrude Jekyll, "is to flaunt and to swagger." So why not pair dahlias with similarly distinctive containers? A half-dozen pale-pink blooms (top) climb from a two-handled Rum Rill art-pottery vase that was first filled with Skimmia japonica 'Rubella.' Martha bought her pussycat-shaped cream pitcher (above) when she was about 10; when her nieces visit, she likes to use it to arrange flowers, especially dahlias, for their bedroom.

For the most uncomplicated, elegant centerpiece, Martha snipped three nearly identical dahlia blooms and set them at different heights—in a sawtooth-patterned compote, an 1880s pressed-glass sugar bowl, and a cut-glass finger bowl. When floating a flower or setting it upon the rim of a cup or small bowl, be sure to leave an inch or so of stem attached so the bloom can continue to drink.

Opulence can be small and easy. Here, blue hydrangea is contrasted with tendrils of chartreuse Amaranthus 'Viridis' in a silver-filigree teapot inset with coral, lapis, and turquoise. Begin by filling a small globe-shaped container with hydrangea; large pompoms may need to be snipped in two to fit. Then, pick Amaranth tendrils from their stalks, and insert among the hydrangea in bunches; if you insert them piece by piece, the arrangement may end up looking too even and less lush.

Sunflowers, smoke-tree leaves, silvery Plectranthus argentatus, and starry chrysanthemums (above) capture the sunset tones of autumn. More formal paired arrangements (opposite) befit Martha's sideboard. Amaranthus, hydrangea, hypericum berries, sedum 'Autumn Joy,' perilla leaves, and clusters of roses were inserted, in that sequence, into jars set inside tole urns.

Fresh from the cutting garden or roadside stand, playful sunflowers and harvest-hued dahlias (right) make bold bouquets. Cut their stems short, and use a frog to hold them in a mixing bowl. Bigger bouquets of sunflowers placed outdoors are ideal for greeting visitors. A mix of sunflowers and black-eyed Susans in an enameled metal urn (below) anchors a stone walkway at Turkey Hill. Flanking the door (opposite), mahogany-red sunflowers sway in antique enamelware pitchers originally used for bathing.

buying sunflowers

The sunflower is the genesis of many garden-variety tall tales, mostly centered on outrageous claims of twenty-five-foot stalks and the like. But one of the best comes from the Mormons. Legend holds that when members left Missouri in the 1830s in search of a place where they could worship freely, the first wagonful scattered sunflower seeds to mark the way. When more wagons followed the summer after, they were guided to their new home in Utah by the trail of blooms. When buying sunflowers, select stems with sturdy green leaves covered with down; reject any with yellowed or faded foliage. Sunflowers have become so popular recently that seed catalogs list not merely one or two but a dozen or more varieties, some looking not much like the classic golden ten-footer. The color range is sometimes more sunset than sunshine, with bronzes and rusts like 'Autumn Beauty Mix' and maroon-reds like 'Velvet Queen' getting lots of attention. "White" sunflowers, particularly 'Italian White,' which is actually the palest shade of yellow, are another hit. Commercial growers produce varieties especially for the cut-flower market—many will last for as long as ten days in water.

Autumn arrangements are by their very nature rich combinations. Explore your garden for inspiration: Take snippings from shrubs and perennial borders; collect fallen leaves. Gather ingredients from farm stands or markets. Sedum, sunflowers, and crocosmia berries (left) add warmth to Martha's Westport kitchen mantel. The cast-iron urn is lined with layers of plastic wrap to make it water-tight. The thick sunflower stems amply fill the container, so a frog is unnecessary. A similar but more lavish display in a soup tureen (opposite) was begun using a wire frog; as more flowers were added, the other stems, not the frog, provided support. The magenta palette includes hydrangea, astilbe, sunflowers, smoke-tree leaves, stock, and roses.

This bright bouquet (right) is the perfect way to turn a relaxed Sunday brunch into a special afternoon. It's a foolproof arrangement: Open your cupboards and choose a pretty water or wine goblet. Fill it with delicate clusters of chartreuse lady's mantle; then tuck in five or six small sunflowers, their stems snipped short. Fill several goblets to decorate a long table, or fill even more to decorate individual tables at a simple country wedding.

Late-season foliage and vegetables offer unusual shapes, colors, and textures. Massed in a glass compote (this page), silver artemisia, deep indigo monkshood, blue salvia, purple globe thistle, and deep-blue agapanthus (or African lily) shimmer above a silver tray. Ornamental kale, pink stock, red ageratum, scented geranium leaves, and tropical green berzillia berries (opposite) are surprisingly sophisticated in three terrine molds. Frame the arrangements with thick kale stalks; then add the remaining ingredients in small clusters.

[winter]

paper-whites

eucalyptus

amaryllis kale

snowdrops

hellebores

bittersweet

rose hips

Even after the first frost, the garden still has its gifts. Take a closer look. Rose hips, berries, and boughs of greenery are all there to bring inside. Add trumpets of forced amaryllis, or perhaps some white flowers—an extravagance from the market. In winter, even a single flower can be uplifting—as much as a big July bouquet. And soon enough, those few unlikely little blooms of late winter will peek through the covering of snow.

White flowers epitomize winter elegance. A five-part arrangement for a buffet (above) uses paper-whites—easy to force in winter—roses, and ornithogalum in silver julep cups. On the desk in Martha's East Hampton bedroom (opposite), loosely styled bursts of white roses, pussy willow, privet berries, acacia foliage, and sea holly fill a pair of large McCoy urns.

Lazy in a cast-iron figural urn, small red amaryllis, variegated ivy leaves, and 'Spring Green' tulips provide traditional holiday colors, but softened by white. Add the tulips last, in groups of three or four, so they won't be lost among the tips of ivy and amaryllis. Without the white and most of the green (opposite), the color red can be used to explore shape, texture, and sheen. Velvety 'Black Magic' roses, parrot tulips, and glistening winterberries are captivating in a landscape of ruby-red blown glass. Resist the urge to make the centers of these arrangements tall: Allow the surface to take on a natural, undulating form; make some of the outer stems the longest.

Amaryllis blossoms (below) get a chance to show off when trimmed from their tall stalks. The same is true for the long-stemmed gooseneck loosestrife slipped into this row of red and white table arrangements. Use complementary small vessels — silver cups or clear glasses — and let the flowers be the stars. Holiday bouquets are just as lovely in less traditional hues, as in a spray (right) of white roses, purple globe thistle, fresh pine, skimmia, and white calla lilies.

hunting for materials

During the bleakest days of winter it's usually necessary to supplement what materials you can gather from the garden — dried or evergreen — with flowers and foliage from the florist shop or flower market. Don't hesitate to try some of the more exotic branches and blossoms you discover as long as their colors, shapes, and textures are suitable to the rest of the arrangement. And don't be afraid to snip off a few stems from the forced paper-whites or amaryllis bulbs on the kitchen windowsill to accent a special holiday centerpiece with fragrance or strokes of color. It's okay to be a little more jubilant, a little more old-fashioned at Christmas. Although things are kept simple the rest of the year, this is the season to pull out all the stops. Some other materials that add interest to winter arrangements are skimmia, acacia, seeded and willow eucalyptus, nerine, hypericum berries, Cyrtanthus lilies, olive, mistletoe, pomegranates, magnolia leaves, and Casablanca lilies. All of these, used judiciously, can evoke the season as readily as poinsettias and amaryllis. Experiment with unusual materials and color combinations. Your own fresh, new decorations will be cause for celebration.

Martha's East Hampton garden yielded these attractive, plump rose hips and prickly branches of barberry foliage in early winter. The cuttings, casually laid in a trio of metal urns, are softened and filled out by stems of downy pink-petaled nerine. Such spiky clippings and delicate flowers lend themselves especially well to low, loose arrangements, perfect for occupying the space on a mantel just below a mirror.

Together, flowers and containers can be planned to create a more important-looking scene. Display a collection of similar vases, but fill only a few with shapely arrangements. Martha's mercury-glass vases (opposite) hold 'Curioso Orientalis' roses, unopened bittersweet, and skimmia. A black ceramic urn (this page) was filled with white ornamental kale, 'Emerald Green' roses, and privet berries. Since the kale fills the urn so densely, this arrangement can be made quickly, without a frog.

The late-winter garden is far
from barren. When a layer of
snow still covers the ground,
snowdrops and hellebores may
emerge as harbingers of spring,
full of temerity. Chartreuse
Helleborus foetidus (below) are
massed in an ironstone food
mold. Their waxy bells, nodding
over the container's edge, are
enchanting. Translucent-white
snowdrops make charming mini
arrangements (right): Place
them in antique juice glasses on
a glass cake pedestal to take
advantage of late-winter light.

rediscovering hellebores

Hellebores have become so popular
recently that the Lenten rose (*H. orientalis*)
and the white-flowered Christmas rose
(*H. niger*) can usually be found among the
shade perennials at many nurseries. They
have been widely enjoyed in English
gardens for many years. Because they were
rarely seen in American gardens, however,
hellebores got a reputation for being
difficult, when they were simply unfamiliar.
The earliest of all blooming perennials,
hellebores are low-growing, handsome
plants that produce flowers in late winter.
These two-inch blossoms, some pointed
at the tips, are often downward-facing
and lost among the foliage. Unless you
are on your hands and knees (or the
hellebores are planted in raised beds), the
best way to appreciate their flowers is in
cut arrangements. Hellebores mix well
in bouquets with tree and shrub cuttings,
but Martha prefers *H. orientalis* in masses
by itself, where its fascinating cup-shaped
blossoms in maroon, pink, white, cream,
red, pale green—including speckled
combinations—can be studied up close.
Hellebores are long-lasting in arrangements,
sometimes persisting up to two weeks.
But beware that all parts of the hellebore
plant, including the seeds, are poisonous.

The shapes of hellebore flowers range from stars to bowls in a variety of colors, including yellow, white, and pink. The green flower in the center glass is H. argutifolius, surrounded by H. orientalis hybrids. Fresh-cut hellebores, exhibited individually or in arrangements, will remind you that your garden will soon be back in bloom.

the guide

Items pictured but not listed are from private collections. Addresses and telephone numbers of sources may change prior to or following publication, as may price and availability of any item.

cover

HAIR AND MAKEUP by Hiromi Kobari for One. CLOTHES styled by Inge Fonteyne with The Agency.

The Basics of Arranging

page 13

1916 STEEL-CAGE FROGS by the Dazey Flower Holder Company, $60 to $90 each, available from Paula Rubenstein Ltd., 65 Prince Street, New York, NY 10012; 212-966-8954.

choosing the right vase

page 19

AMETHYST-GLASS TUMBLER, $65, from L. Becker Flowers, 217 East 83rd Street, New York, NY 10028; 212-439-6001. SILVER-PLATED VASE from David Stypmann Co., 190 Sixth Avenue, New York, NY 10013; 212-226-5717.

conditioning cut flowers

page 23

FELCO PRUNERS (GFP001), $45, and 7"-by-12" PAINTED FLOWER BUCKET (GFB002), $38 (available in three sizes), available from Martha By Mail, 800-950-7130 or www.marthabymail.com. Free catalog. GALVANIZED WATERING CAN, available from Pottery Barn, 212-579-8477 for store locations. FLORIST KNIFE (#422A06), $15.95, available from Dorothy Biddle Service,

348 Greeley Lake Road, Greeley, PA 18425; 570-226-3239.

pages 24–26

FLORIST KNIFE (#422A06), $15.95, available from Dorothy Biddle Service, 348 Greeley Lake Road, Greeley, PA 18425; 570-226-3239. JAPANESE GARDEN SHEARS, $22, available from Takashimaya, 693 Fifth Avenue, New York, NY 10022; 212-350-0100 or 800-753-2038. FELCO PRUNERS (GFP001), $45, and 4¹/₄"-high PRESSED-GLASS FLOWERPOT (GFV003), $28 for set of 2 (available in three sizes), both available from Martha By Mail, 800-950-7130 or marthabymail.com. Free catalog.

page 25

ROGARD PROFESSIONAL FLORAL PRESERVATIVE, $5 for 12 ounces of concentrate, available from the Cook's Garden, P.O. Box 535, Londonderry, VT 05148; 800-457-9703.

building a sturdy foundation

pages 29–34

FLOWER-ARRANGING KIT (CFA001), $55, available from Martha By Mail, 800-950-7130 or www.marthabymail.com. Free catalog. FLOWER-ARRANGING SUPPLIES available from: B&J Floral, 103 West 28th Street, New York, NY 10001; 212-564-6086. Country House Floral Supply, P.O. Box 853, Eastham, MA 02642; 508-255-6664. Free catalog. Dorothy Biddle Service, 348 Greeley Lake Road, Greeley, PA 18425; 570-226-3239. Free catalog.

planting a cutting garden

pages 37–43

MAIL-ORDER FLOWER SEEDS available from:

W. Atlee Burpee, 300 Park Avenue, Warminster, PA 18974; 800-888-1447. The Cook's Garden, P.O. Box 535, Londonderry, VT 05148; 802-824-3400. Johnny's Selected Seeds, Foss Hill Road, Albion, ME 04910; 207-437-4395. Park Seed Co., Cokesbury Road, Greenwood, SC 29647; 800-845-3369. Select Seeds Antique Flowers, 180 Stickney Road, Union, CT 06076; 860-684-9310. Catalog, $3. Shepherd's Garden Seeds, 30 Irene Street, Torrington, CT 06790; 860-482-3638. Stokes Seeds, Box 548, Buffalo, NY 14240; 716-695-6980. Thompson & Morgan, P.O. Box 1308, Jackson, NJ 08527; 800-274-7333.

Bouquets Throughout the Year

spring

page 50

AMERICAN MATTE-WHITE ROADSIDE POTTERY and FLUTED FLORIST VASE from U.S.E.D., 17 Perry Street, New York, NY 10014; 212-627-0730.

page 53

MAGNOLIA VARIETIES available from: Gossler Farms Nursery, 1200 Weaver Road, Springfield, OR 97478; 541-746-3922. Catalog with 110 varieties, $2. Greer Gardens, 1280 Goodpasture Island Road, Eugene, OR 97401; 800-548-0111. Catalog with multiple varieties, $3. Louisiana Nursery, 5835 Highway 182, Opelousas, LA 70570; 318-948-3696. Catalog with 500 varieties, $6. FOR MORE INFORMATION ABOUT MAGNOLIAS, contact Roberta Hagen of the Magnolia Society, 6616 81st Street, Cabin John, MD 20818; 301-320-4296 or rhagen6920@aol.com.

pages 56–59

DAFFODIL BULBS available from: W. Atlee

Burpee, 300 Park Avenue, Warminster, PA 18974; 800-888-1447. Free catalog. The Daffodil Mart, 800-255-2852. Free catalog. McClure & Zimmerman, Box 368, Friesland, WI 53935; 920-326-4220. Free catalog. K. Van Bourgondien & Sons, 800-552-9996. Free catalog. Van Engelen Inc., 23 Tulip Drive, Bantam, CT 06750; 860-567-8734. Free catalog. FOR MORE INFORMATION ABOUT DAFFODILS, contact Naomi Liggett at the American Daffodil Society, 4126 Winfield Road, Columbus, OH 43220; 614-451-4747.

page 56

MCCOY POTTERY available from: Fritz's American Wonder at the Tomato Factory, 2 Somerset Street, Hopewell, NJ 08525; 609-466-9833. Sage Street Antiques, Sage Street and Route 114, Sag Harbor, NY 11963; 516-725-4036.

pages 60–63

TULIP BULBS available from: K. Van Bourgondien & Sons, 800-552-9916. Free catalog. Van Engelen Inc., 23 Tulip Drive, Bantam, CT 06750; 860-567-8734. Free catalog. White Flower Farm, 860-496-9624 or 800-503-9624. Free catalog.

pages 64 and 65

LILY OF THE VALLEY PIPS available from: W. Atlee Burpee, 300 Park Avenue, Warminster, PA 18974; 800-888-1447. Free catalog. Park Seed, 1 Parkton Avenue, Greenwood, SC 29647; 800-845-3369. Free catalog. Shepherd's Garden Seeds, 30 Irene Street, Torrington, CT 06790; 860-482-3638. Free catalog.

pages 66–69

VIOLETS available from: Gardens of the Blue Ridge, Box 10, Pineola, NC 28662; 828-733-2417. Catalog, $3. Lamb Nurseries, 101 East Sharp Avenue, Spokane, WA 99202; 509-328-7956. Catalog, $1.50. Logee's Greenhouses, 141 North Street, Danielson, CT 06239; 860-774-8038. Catalog $3. Wayside Gardens, 1 Garden Lane, Hodges, SC 29695; 800-845-1124. Free catalog. FOR MORE INFORMATION ABOUT VIOLETS, contact the International Violet Association, 8604 Main Road, Berlin Heights, OH 44814. Free newsletter.

pages 70 and 71

LILAC VARIETIES available from: Congdon &

Weller Nursery, P.O. Box 1507, 10308 Mile Block Road, North Collins, NY 14111; 716-337-0171. Free catalog. Heard Gardens, 5355 Merle Hay Road, Johnston, IA 50131; 515-276-4533 or www.heardgardens.com. Catalog, $2.

summer

pages 74–77

PEONY PLANTS available from Klehm Nursery, 4210 North Duncan Road, Champaign, IL 61822; 800-553-3715. Free catalog.

pages 78 and 79

LILY BULBS, $3 to $7, available from the Lily Garden, P.O. Box 407, La Center, WA 98629; 360-263-5588. (Tuesday through Thursday, 9 A.M. to 12 P.M., P.T.) Free catalog.

pages 82 and 83

IRIS VARIETIES available from: Cooley's Gardens, Box 126MS (11553 Silverton Road NE), Silverton, OR 97381; 800-225-5391 or 503-873-5463. Long's Gardens, 3240 Broadway, Boulder, CO 80304; 303-442-2353. McMillen's Iris Gardens, RR1, Norwich, Ontario, Canada NOJ 1PO; 519-468-6508. Roris Gardens, 8195 Bradshaw Road, Sacramento, CA 95829; 916-689-7460 or www.jps.net/roris.com. Schreiner's Iris Gardens, 3625 Quinaby Road NE, Salem, OR 97303; 800-525-2367. Catalog, $5.

pages 84–86

ALLIUMS available from: the Daffodil Mart, 30 Irene Street, Torrington, CT 06790; 800-255-2852. Free catalog. Heronswood Nursery, 7530 NE 288th Street, Kingston, WA 98346; 360-297-4172. Catalog $5.

pages 87–90

POPPY SEEDS available from: the Cook's Garden, Box 535, Londonderry, VT 05148; 802-824-3400. Park Seed Co., 800-845-3369. Thompson & Morgan, P.O. Box 1308, Jackson, NJ 08527; 800-274-7333. POPPY SEEDLINGS available from K. Van Bourgondien & Sons, Box 1000, 245 Farmingdale Road, Babylon, NY 11702; 516-669-3520.

pages 92–101

ROSES available from: Heirloom Old Garden Roses, 24062 NE Riverside Drive, St. Paul, OR 97137; 503-538-1576. Catalog $5.

Pickering Nurseries, 670 Kingston Road, Pickering, Ontario, Canada L1V 1A6; 905-839-2111. Catalog, $3. Roses of Yesterday, 831-728-1901 or www.rosesofyesterday.com. Wayside Gardens, 1 Garden Lane, Hodges, SC 29695; 800-845-1124. Free catalog.

pages 102 and 103

SWEET-PEA SEEDS available from: Select Seeds Antique Flowers, 180 Stickney Road, Union, CT 06076; 860-684-9310. Catalog, $3. Thompson & Morgan, P.O. Box 1308, Jackson, NJ 08527; 800-274-7333. Free catalog.

pages 104 and 105

CUT FRESH AND DRIED HYDRANGEAS, $16 for bunch of 6, from Green Valley Growers, 10450 Cherry Ridge Road, Sebastopol, CA 95472; 707-823-5583. HYDRANGEA SHRUBS available from Greer Gardens, 1280 Goodpasture Island Road, Eugene, OR 97401; 541-686-8266. Catalog, $3.

pages 106 and 107; 109

GLADIOLUS CORMS available from: Kingfisher Glads, 11734 Road 33.5, Madera, CA 93638; 209-645-5329. Free catalog. Waushara Gardens, N5491 Fifth Drive, Plainfield, WI 54966; 715-335-4462.

page 107

POTTERY VASES available from the Lively Set, 33 Bedford Street, New York, NY 10014; 212-807-8417.

pages 108–110

ZINNIA SEEDS available from: W. Atlee Burpee, 300 Park Avenue, Warminster, PA 18974; 800-888-1447. Free catalog. Park Seed Co., Cokesbury Road, Greenwood, SC 29647; 800-845-3369. Free catalog. Southern Exposure Seed Exchange, P.O. Box 170, Earlysville, VA 22936; 804-973-4703 or www.southernexposure.com. Catalog, $2.

page 111

SNAPDRAGON SEEDS available from: W. Atlee Burpee, 300 Park Avenue, Warminster, PA 18974; 800-888-1447. Thompson & Morgan, P.O. Box 1308, Jackson, NJ 08527; 800-274-7333. BLOWN-GLASS VASES from L. Becker Flowers, 217 East 83rd Street, New York, NY 10028; 212-439-6001.

autumn

pages 114–116

DAHLIA TUBERS available from: Garden Valley Dahlias, 406 Lower Garden Valley Road, Roseburg, OR 97470; 541-673-8521. Free catalog with more than 200 varieties. Swan Island Dahlias, P.O. Box 700, Canby, OR 97013; 503-266-7711. Catalog with more than 200 varieties, $3.

pages 117 and 118; 123

CUT FRESH AND DRIED HYDRANGEAS, $16 for bunch of 6, from Green Valley Growers, 10450 Cherry Ridge Road, Sebastopol, CA 95472; 707-823-5583. HYDRANGEA SHRUBS available from Greer Gardens, 1280 Good-pasture Island Road, Eugene, OR 97401; 541-686-8266. Catalog, $3.

pages 119–123

SUNFLOWER SEEDS available from: the Cook's Garden, P.O. Box 535, Londonderry, VT 05148; 802-824-3400. Johnny's Selected Seeds, Foss Hill Road, Albion, ME 04910; 207-437-4301. Park Seed Co., Cokesbury Road, Greenwood, SC 29647; 800-845-3369. Shepherd's Garden Seeds, 30 Irene Street, Torrington, CT 06790; 860-482-3638. Smith & Hawken, 2 Arbor Lane, P.O. Box 6900, Florence, KY 41022; 800-776-3336. Free catalog. Southern Exposure Seed Exchange, P.O. Box 170, Earlysville, VA 22936; 804-973-4703 or www.southernexposure.com. Catalog, $2. Stokes Seeds, Box 548, Buffalo, NY 14240; 716-695-6980. Thompson & Morgan, P.O. Box 1308, Jackson, NJ 08527; 800-274-7333.

page 120

DAHLIA TUBERS available from: Garden Valley Dahlias, 406 Lower Garden Valley Road, Roseburg, OR 97470; 541-673-8521. Free catalog with more than 200 varieties. Swan Island Dahlias, P.O. Box 700, Canby, OR 97013; 503-266-7711. Catalog with more than 200 varieties, $3.

winter

page 131

BLOWN-GLASS VASE and BOWL from L. Becker Flowers, 217 East 83rd Street, New York, NY 10028; 212-439-6001.

pages 136 and 137

HELLEBORE VARIETIES available (mail order) from: Gossler Farms Nursery, 1200 Weaver Road, Springfield, OR 97478; 541-746-3922. Catalog, $2. Greer Gardens, 1280 Good Pasture Island Road, Eugene, OR 97401; 800-548-0111. Catalog, $3. Heronswood Nursery, 7530 NE 288th Street, Kingston, WA 98346; 360-297-4172. Catalog, $5. Roslyn Nursery, 211 Burrs Lane, Dix Hills, NY 11746; 516-643-9347. Catalog, $3. HELLEBORE VARIETIES also available (no mail order) from: Molbak's Nursery, 13625 NE 175th Street, Woodinville, WA 98072; 425-483-5000. Wells Medina Nursery, 8300 NE 24th Street, Medina, WA 98039; 425-454-1853.

If you have enjoyed this book, please join us as a subscriber to MARTHA STEWART LIVING magazine. The annual subscription rate is $26 for ten issues. Call toll-free 800-999-6515, or visit our web site, www.marthastewart.com.

contributors

A special thanks to Margaret Roach, the gardening editor of MARTHA STEWART LIVING, and to the many photographers, art directors, editors, and stylists whose inspirational ideas contributed to this volume, notably Stephen Drucker, James Dunlinson, Necy Fernandes, Kathleen Hackett, Joelle Hoverson, Melissa Morgan, Eric A. Pike, Heidi J. Posner, Scot Schy, Kevin Sharkey, and Gael Towey. Thanks also to the entire staff of Martha Stewart Living Omnimedia and to everyone at Oxmoor House, Clarkson Potter, Satellite Graphics, and Quebecor Printing whose work and dedication helped produce this book.

Photography

William Abranowicz
pages 5, 10, 20, 21, 30, 64, 65 (left), 77, 83, 84, 90 (bottom), 92, 103, 108, 119, 122 (bottom), 123, 125, 128, 130, 131, 133–135

Ruven Afanador
page 50 (bottom)

Anthony Amos
page 59 (right)

Michel Arnaud
pages 37–40, 42 (left, top and bottom), 43 (top right)

Christopher Baker
pages 16 (right), 61, 106 (bottom), 107

Anita Calero
page 13 (top left)

Beatriz DaCosta
page 81

Reed Davis
pages 6 (bottom left), 15, 23, 24, 25 (all but far right), 26, 27, 43 (top left), 79, 80, 96 (left), 97 (bottom), 111 (bottom right), 115 (bottom right)

Todd Eberle
pages 3, 13 (top right; bottom), 29, 31–33, 70, 71 (bottom), 76 (left), 82 (top), 88, 89, 90 (top), 91, 97 (top), 100 (bottom), 102

Richard Felber
pages 7 (left), 8, 44, 47 (top left), 73, 105

Don Freeman
page 71 (top)

Dana Gallagher
pages 2, 6 (top left), 17, 19, 25 (far right), 34 (bottom row), 35, 43 (bottom), 50 (top), 51–55, 56 (top), 57, 58, 62, 63, 65 (bottom right), 78, 93, 96 (right), 104 (left), 109, 114, 115 (left; top right), 116–118, 120, 121, 122 (top), 124, 129, 132, 136

Gentl & Hyers
page 60 (bottom)

Kit Latham
pages 42 (right), 106 (top)

Stephen Lewis
pages 65 (top right), 104 (right)

Amy Neunsinger
pages 16 (left, top and bottom), 34 (top row), 68 (left), 69, 74, 75 (top), 76 (right), 82 (bottom), 87, 98, 110, 111 (left; top right)

Victoria Pearson
front cover, pages 75 (bottom), 99, back cover

Randy Plimpton
pages 7 (right), 47 (bottom), 127

Maria Robledo
page 56 (bottom)

Victor Schrager
pages 7 (center), 66, 67, 86, 113

Evan Sklar
pages 6 (right), 9, 47 (top right), 49, 59 (left), 85

Jonelle Weaver
page 137

Elizabeth Zeschin
pages 4, 60 (top), 68 (right), 94, 95, 100 (top), 101

Illustration

Melissa Sweet
page 41

index